UTM made me do this.

Yoshi helped.

T0019508

A Love Song, A Death Rattle, A Battle Cry

Kyle "Guante" Tran Myhre

A LOVE SONG, A DEATH RATTLE, A BATTLE CRY

Kyle "Guante" Tran Myhre

With a foreword by Saymoukda "Refugenius" Vongsay

© 2016 Kyle "Guante" Tran Myhre
2nd Edition, 2017

Published by Button Poetry / Exploding Pinecone Press
Minneapolis, MN 55403 | http://www.buttonpoetry.com

All rights reserved.
Manufactured in the United States of America
Cover Design: Nikki Clark
ISBN 978-1-943-73533-4

LINKS:
www.guante.info
www.twitter.com/elguante
www.facebook.com/guantesolo
www.instagram.com/guantesolo
www.guante.tumblr.com
www.youtube.com/tripguante

LISTEN:
Guante: A Furious Vexation (2017)
Guante & Katrah-Quey: Post-Post-Race (2016)
Guante: A Love Song, A Death Rattle, A Battle Cry (2015) Sifu Hotman:
Embrace the Sun (2014)
Guante: Dungeons (2014)
Guante & Big Cats: You Better Weaponize (2012)
Guante & Claire de Lune: A Loud Heart (2011)
Guante & Big Cats: Don't Be Nice (2010)
Guante & Big Cats: An Unwelcome Guest (2010)

CONTENTS

SONGS

FOREWORD

I don't normally do this: penning forewords for books.

Here's what I know: that sometimes we have to be forward in order to keep it moving forward. Whether we are one voice, a handful, or a million—if we do not speak with conviction, honesty, and oftentimes through vulnerability, we might not progress.

A Love Song, A Death Rattle, A Battle Cry contains a body of work that does not confine to one identifier, not because the boxes to mark off on the list weren't clear, but because the words, more importantly— in whatever literary form they took—are interrogative. For instance, they ask you to rethink your perceptions on what it means to live in a sex-coded society or recheck your relationship to the white/brown/ black/yellow faces in your immediate life.

In *Cherry Spoon Bridge to Nowhere*, I'm asked, "Where are you?" I'm an optimist so I will tell you that I am where there are radio programs with voices that match my mother's, where on any given weekend a poet who resembles my best friend is headlining, where there is a mosque in Little Mekong, and where there are police officers and elected officials who were raised in the same housing projects as me. These *are days I forget the dirt underneath the endless white of winter.* But we are here. We are backpackers, grocery cart wranglers, teaching artists, and zombie apocalypse survivors. We are here and we are not dirt. We are not insignificant. We can all be change-makers and progress-instigators.

If you think it's hard, that's because you're not really trying. AMIRIGHT? In *A Series of Essays on Media*, we meet the Political Correctness Police and eight of the most common invalid arguments regarding pop culture and offensiveness that have been asked. As hard as it can be sometimes, we have to answer, unwavering, no quivers in our voices. It may be difficult at first but keep trying and doing.

This is not an official manual on how to dismantle sexism, rape culture, white privilege, police brutality, and coming-off-as-racist large institutions for the performing arts. It's a resource. It's one person's voice that will hopefully incite you to decapitate (not literally, of course; we're not monsters) all of the sea witches before they convince you to give up your voices.

We might not know what the sum of our voices and our actions will be, but we will be fucked if we ever stop being forward, moving forward.

A Love Song, A Death Rattle, A Battle Cry is a time capsule that will be relevant decades from now. This shit is urgent and Guante is the catalyst we all deserve. #NotSorryThatImNotSorry

Saymoukda "Refugenius" Vongsay

Editor's note: find more of Saymoukda's work here:
www.saymoukdatherefugenius.com

If I had a dime for every happy poem I wrote
I'd be dead

—ED BOK LEE, "Poetry Is a Sickness"

TEN THINGS EVERYONE SHOULD KNOW ABOUT SPOKEN WORD AND SLAM POETRY

A very common piece of advice in spoken word workshops or critique circles is "just do the poem." So many of us, especially when we're just starting out, instinctually want to frame, contextualize, or introduce the poem. This manifests as any number of statements like "this is just something I wrote when..." or "this isn't really done; I'm not sure if it has a title yet, but..." or even "this is terrible but I'm going to share it anyway," etc.

That advice—to dive in, with no disclaimers or introductions—is partly about acknowledging the dramatic effect of a poem that starts from silence, from breath. It is also partly about calming the performer down, allowing their work to simply exist, as it is, with no apologies. Especially in poetry slam spaces—you only have three minutes, so there isn't really time for "artist statements."

That being said, I love contextualizing poems. The more that I've moved away from slams and toward performing hour-long sets, the more I've grown to appreciate the power that can come from framing notes, artist statements, and organic dialogue with the audience. We all listen and learn in different ways and those fourth wall-breaking moments can sometimes be as meaningful as the poems themselves.

In that spirit, I wanted to include an introduction to this book that both contextualizes my poems and offers an introduction to the form—and culture—of spoken word for anyone who may not already be part of that community.

Of course, this list is not about capturing all of spoken word and slam poetry culture in one piece of writing; part of the beauty of our community is that we don't all agree on everything, and the work that we do is fluid, dynamic, and impacted by context, identities, and intertwining thought-currents.

What follows is more so an illumination of a few pet peeves and misconceptions that I run across all the time. Though I'm no voice-of-God authority on this subject, I am a practitioner; my hope is that this piece can add additional clarity, depth, and nuance to the ongoing conversation.

1. Words Mean Things: A Point About Terminology

This is a can of worms, so I'm not going to to attempt to provide the ultimate, catch-all definition of *spoken word* here. I will, however, share the framework that I use when it comes to terms:

- **"Spoken Word"** is an umbrella term. It refers to poetry that is read aloud; it may contain elements of theater, stand-up comedy, storytelling, rhetoric, jazz, hip hop, or other forms. We could go deeper with this, in terms of the difference between "recitation" and "performance," or the difference between creating work that is meant to be performed vs. work that is about the page first and then happens to be performed (and how each approach impacts the writing itself), but I think this is a good starting point. You could also potentially use the term **"performance poetry."**

- **"Slam Poetry"** is often used interchangeably with "spoken word," but I would argue that it means something more specific: slam poetry is spoken word performed at a poetry slam (more on that later). While there may be certain tropes or approaches that are more common in slam poetry than in other kinds of spoken word, the real difference is not about form—it's about context.

- **"Beat Poetry"** refers to the poetry of the Beat Generation, whose work is now 50+ years old. Please do not call a 20- year-old spoken word artist a "beat poet" unless that's some kind of explicit shtick they're running with. The stereotypical imagery of berets and bongo drums is simply not what spoken word is today.

- **"Spoken Slam Hip Hop Beat Jams"** is not a real thing. Additionally, I was once called a "slap poet," though that was probably a typo. Probably.

2. Spoken Word is Poetry, Whether You Like It or Not

Of course, we don't all have to be on the same page regarding our enjoyment of or appreciation for spoken word. But to say that "it isn't poetry" (as many do, with gusto) is closed-minded and, frankly, ahistorical. After all, the history in which poetry was primarily about the page is shorter than the history in which poetry was primarily oral (see next point).

Furthermore, I can't help but notice the racist and classist undertones in the bizarrely narrow definition of poetry that so many hold on to so desperately; I am interested in asking why that narrow definition (the one that says that poetry *must* rhyme, or be metered, or be published, or follow established rules) persists in the minds of so many. Where does that definition come from? Who benefits from it?

Now, this does not mean that I believe that all spoken word is to aunthu und parfect and amazing. For every spoken word piece that I love, I can think of another (or five) that I despise. The argument here isn't that we shouldn't have standards; it's that we should think critically about the history of those standards, and who has had access to the spaces in which they were created.

Finally, it is also helpful to note that the "page/stage" divide is an artificial one. Lots of great spoken word artists are published poets, award-winners and professors. Lots of page poets are very good at performing their work. As different as spoken word and written poetry can be in many regards, there's still an enormous overlap.

3. Spoken Word is Old, and New, but Mostly Old

Even though spoken word is very often characterized as a new, underground artistic phenomenon, or as a novel, radical reconceptualization of the relationship between poetry and its audience, it's important to note that spoken word has been around for as long as language has. It is one of the oldest artistic practices that we have. The griot, the storyteller, the person responsible for orally passing down information from generation to generation: every culture on earth has some kind of analogue to this. The *Iliad* and *Odyssey* were spoken word poems. We can trace the current spoken word boom back through the Black Arts Movement, the Beat Generation, the Harlem Renaissance, deeper and deeper into history, and we'll get to the griot.

And sure—when most people today talk about "spoken word," they're referring to the 30 year-old manifestation of the practice driven by poetry slams, Def Poetry Jam, and viral videos. But it is important to know that this art has deeper roots, and that those of us who do this are taking part—knowingly or not—in a much older cultural practice.

4. Spoken Word is Big and Diverse

I understand that for a lot of people, slam poetry is a punchline. The stereotype of the grim, ultra-earnest college kid shouting clichés about how "the man" is corrupt, in a forced rhythm, while a dozen people in a coffee shop snap their fingers, is deeply embedded in pop culture.

But I've been performing in poetry slams, traveling around the country for spoken word shows, and watching poetry online for a decade now, and one thing that always strikes me is how authentically diverse the community is. After all, a fundamental pillar of the culture is the idea that everyone has a story, and every story matters. People approach spoken word from all walks of life, from all identities, and from a myriad of approaches to the form. I would say that the culture is largely driven by young people, and young people of color especially, but it is by no means dominated by a singular voice.

The attitude that "spoken word all sounds the same" is similar to the attitude that "all jazz is just random notes and gesticulating," or "all hip hop is just shouting about guns," or "all photography is just high-contrast black-and-white portraits of elderly people." While there are common tropes and shared delivery tactics (which is true in any form), those elements exist within a framework that allows for endless variations and stylistic impulses. This leads into the next point:

5. Spoken Word is Democratic, and Yes, That Means That Some of It is Bad

Another fundamental pillar of spoken word culture is the idea that poetry is for everyone. Anyone can be a poet. Anyone can serve as a judge at a slam. Anyone can sit in the audience and decide what they like or don't like. It isn't about what MFA program you got into, or how many poems you've gotten published, or who co-signs you; it's about how we build community with one another through the telling of our stories and the sharing of our words.

What this means in practice is that no matter who you are, or how much experience or training you have, you can sign up at an open mic or poetry slam and share something. So of course, if you're an audience member at some random open mic, you are not guaranteed two hours of brilliant writing. A lot of spoken word is pretty bad. But the larger point here is that most *art* is pretty bad— we just might not ever experience the "bad" indie rock, visual art, dance, etc. The spoken word community, however, is intentionally set up in such a way where the great and not-so-great exist in the same spaces. And though I've sat through many a not-so-great slam, I would still argue that this is a very positive thing.

The spoken word community includes icons like Andrea Gibson and Saul Williams, right alongside some 15-year-old kid performing at their very first open mic. It includes Marc Bamuthi Joseph's boundary-pushing spoken word theater work, right alongside a part-time bartender who competes in poetry slams for a little extra money. It includes the best writers I know—Patricia Smith, Bao Phi, Suheir Hammad, etc.—*and* countless people who are just starting out, or still growing, or trying to figure out what they have to say. It's about process *and* product. It's about the function of art beyond the art itself. This is immeasurably valuable, and part of why spoken word represents something deeper than just another hobby or literary/artistic movement.

6. Spoken Word is Bigger than Poetry Slams

A poetry slam is a poetry reading staged as an Olympic-style competition. Five judges are picked randomly from the crowd, poets perform, and the judges give those poets scores based on content, form, delivery, originality, or whatever they want. It's silly, and most of the people who participate know that it's not really about the points; it's about getting the audience engaged. Still, slams are popular all over the US (and beyond), and have become the focal point for spoken word's resurgence.

Although the competitive element turns a lot of people off, I like poetry slams. I like the symbolism of them: write for the people. Write something that connects. Have fun. I like that the judges are random weirdos and not creative writing professors or literary critics. Everything in points #4 and #5 comes alive at the poetry slam. Slams aren't perfect, and there are important conversations to be had about the intersections of competition, art, identity, and trauma, but I still believe that they are valuable.

That being said, it is important to note here that spoken word happens in other spaces too, and that a lot of the value of slam is that it is one outlet among many. For those of us who grew up in the slam world, it can be too easy to forget that slam is just one way to participate, and that participating *solely* through slam can be unhealthy (and/or just boring). You can find spoken word at open mics, themed readings, political rallies, classrooms, social justice education programs, churches, punk shows, prisons, and many other spaces too.

7. Spoken Word and Hip Hop Are Not the Same

I've heard people talk about how spoken word is just another element of hip hop. I've also heard people talk about how hip hop grew out of the work of early spoken word pioneers like the Last Poets and Gil Scott-Heron. I would say that there is truth in both statements, but also that both statements make it easy to oversimplify the relationship. I think that hip hop and spoken word—as both art forms and cultures—have been in dialogue with one another for the past few decades, but also that neither one is wholly indebted to the other. They overlap—in terms of audience, artists, roots, styles, and approaches—but they are also *distinct* cultures and communities.

This comes up in conversations about form. Students ask me all the time: "what's the difference between rapping and spoken word?" There's a deeper conversation we can have there, but in short, I think of rapping as a specific kind of poetry; and like any poetic form (haiku, sonnet, etc.), it has rules. Rapping rhymes. It is performed at a set tempo and rhythm. It is performed over music. Spoken word, on the other hand, can rhyme, but doesn't have to. It can be performed to a set tempo and rhythm, but doesn't have to be. It can be performed over music, but it doesn't have to be. There are fewer formal guidelines with spoken word and slam poetry. But in terms of substance—you can rap about anything, and you can write a poem about anything.

Of course, both spoken word and hip hop are about speaking truth to power, and lifting up the voices and narratives that are so often silenced in our society. Both are about the implicitly political act of a human being standing on a stage and saying *something* to a hundred other human beings (especially when you, and/or that audience, hold identities that are misrepresented in the broader culture). Like I said, there is overlap. But where the casual observer might just see *"urban youth* saying stuff into a mic" and assume that the two forms are exactly the same, I would encourage us all to have a more nuanced view of their similarities, differences, and histories, in order to pay the proper respect to both.

8. Spoken Word Does Not Have to Be Political, But There Might Be a Reason for Why So Much of It Is

Again, there are no rules with spoken word, beyond the fact that poetry slams have three-minute time limits. This applies to form, but also to substance. A poet can write and perform about any topic they want. Of course, the stereotype is that all spoken word is ranting about the revolution; and to be sure, poetry slams generally do feature a lot more poems about identity, power, oppression, struggle, and politics than poems about trees or "pure" lyrical experiments.

Part of the reason for this, I would argue, is that as much as spoken word *is* poetry, it is also something more. It's a public forum for people to get together and have the conversations that we so often don't get to have in our everyday lives. It's a platform to say something that means something to you in front of a hundred strangers. And when so many spoken word practitioners are young people, and/or people holding oppressed identities, and/or people with voices that have just generally not been valued (or even noticed) in society, it shouldn't surprise anyone that so much spoken word is political. It should be. It needs to be.

9. Spoken Word is Not a Fad; It's Growing

Every few months, someone publishes another "Is Poetry Dead?" essay. I understand why—it's click-bait, and there are certainly valid arguments to be made on both sides of the debate regarding aesthetic populism, outreach to new audiences, the accessibility of MFA programs and other weighty topics. The problem, however, is how the question is framed: poetry is dead because fewer people buy poetry books or read poetry journals, or poetry is dead because it's stylistically stagnant, or poetry is dead because it doesn't have a presence in the upper echelons of American media or culture.

Left out of these equations, due to either simple ignorance or a willful distaste for the form (and its practitioners), is spoken word. Even the inevitable response essays and counterpoints that talk about how poetry is still vibrant and important almost always ignore spoken word. And spoken word is very much where poetry is thriving right now.

At the time of this writing, Button Poetry (the biggest distributor of spoken word videos online) has a YouTube channel with more than a half million subscribers and well over a hundred million views. And they're just *one* channel. Even using myself as an example: my work has nearly two million YouTube views, and I make my living as a touring poet traveling around the country. When I do that traveling, I notice spoken word clubs sprouting up at just about every college and high school that I visit, as well as poetry slams in cities across the country generating big energetic crowds.

Which is all to say: this movement is popular and still growing. Especially when thinking about Button and its impact on thousands of people around the world: spoken word is making people (especially young people) excited about poetry. Its viral boom is sparking a new generation of writers, poets, performers, and storytellers—all of whom may start with poetry slams, but then branch into theater, publishing, music, or other arenas. We're still in the middle of that ripple effect.

10. You Can Do This Too, If You Want; Spoken Word is About Community

One of the running themes here is that spoken word is about *us*, more than it's about me, or you, or whatever poet has the most YouTube views. It is a participatory culture. While I make a living as a spoken word poet (along with a growing handful of others), it is important to understand that you don't have to go "all in" to do this. Most spoken word poets have day jobs. Most never go viral. Most don't win every poetry slam that they enter. And this should be celebrated. We don't need more professional poets; we need more cab drivers, teachers, nurses, organizers, and service workers who *write poetry*.

I can imagine someone reading this and saying "easier said than done." And sure, performing in front of people isn't always easy. To support anyone who might be interested, I've tried to collect a few resources at my website (www.guante.info), including a video series of tips, tools, and tactics for aspiring spoken word poets, a list of all of the open mics and poetry slams in my community, a list of 100+ favorite poems by other artists, and more. It might be a matter of finding the space first—a local open mic, an online community, even just an informal writing circle of three or four friends. From there, it's about diving in, having fun, and figuring out what you want to contribute. Let's build.

POEMS

Using the previous essay as context, readers may notice that my relationship with my poems *as poems* is complex. While I have studied poetry (formally and informally) for much of my life, I think of the writings here as performance art pieces first, and poems second. So this book is less "a book of my poems," and more "a book of transcripts of my spoken word work." I've included the text the way it was written: paragraph form, with minimal enjambment or textual flourishes. I'd encourage you to watch the performances as well—they are all available, for free, at my website and on YouTube.

This book is also an opportunity to explore the power of juxtaposition and impressionistic learning. To bring that idea down to earth: I'm an album person. I like songs, but I love how a dozen songs can play off one another and add up to something that is even more powerful than the sum of its parts. Putting these poems next to each other for the first time, outside of my performances—will hopefully illuminate some interesting connections. To that end, some of the poems here will also be accompanied by supplementary essays, and a larger bank of essays is included at the end of this book.

Finally, this book is a way for me to, in a sense, exorcise these poems and look to the future with a clean slate. In terms of context, the bulk of this book was written between about 2005 and 2015. With some of these poems (and especially with some of the essays) I'm both happy to include them here, and happy to note that my writing has grown a lot since they were written. But again: *no disclaimers. Just dive in.*

SMALL TALK

When my girlfriend's parents ask me what I do for a living...

I pull a straight razor out of my back pocket. And I don't tell them that I'm a poet; I sure as hell don't tell them that I'm an MC. I just pull a straight razor out of my back pocket.

And sure: I could lie. I could say that I'm a pilot, or a teacher, or a handsome man, or the *change that I want to see in the world*, or a pipe-smoking grad student. I could go on and on about all the locked doors I can open, or the exotic locales that have crawled up my nose, or the blinding glossiness of my résumé paper.

But I don't. I pull a straight razor out of my back pocket.

Sure: maybe this is overly dramatic. But I've never been very good at small talk. I'm always too busy wondering where interesting scars come from; too busy asking myself how many poorly aimed arrows, casual brushes of skin, drownings, and split seconds of eye contact, over the past ten thousand years, have constructed this moment; too busy imagining the soundtrack to my life dominated by smiling, adult contemporary alterna-rockers, and saying *no*.

Give me hip hop, dressed in leather, knuckles cracking. Give me whatever the opposite of novocain is; let it pulse beneath my skin.

Because we could talk about the weather; that's easy. We could deaden our colors and round our jagged corners so that we may fit more precisely into our own carry-on luggage. I could rattle off a string of pop culture references, and we'd all have a good laugh; but I don't. I pull a straight razor out of my back pocket.

And just as her father begins to say: *sooo, you're a barber?*

I slice my little finger off.

They jump back, instantly, like characters in a poorly edited student film, their lines caught between their teeth, their eyes staring directly into the camera. Levitating with pain, I pick my discarded digit up from off the Olive Garden floor, and with the black sharpie that I always keep in my other back pocket, I write my name on it, and I say:

Give me ten dollars and I will let you keep this.

Not the finger. The moment. Give me ten dollars as tribute to the truth that we once stood here, that I did something worth remembering; that you, on this day, witnessed something larger than traffic, or storm clouds, or time passing.

For the price of a fancy breakfast, press your fingertips to the wet cement of my tombstone. Stand in the background of my iconography. It's only ten dollars; tell my bones they've done a good job keeping me upright; tell yourself that *this* day did not blur by, that this journal entry would be more than an absent-minded doodle. For ten dollars, I will carve my initials into your brainstem.

What do I do for a living?

...I am a poet. An MC. An artist. I am a turtle without a shell, and I have the scars to prove it. I am pulling *myself* from the magician's hat, night after night, and I have the scars to prove it. I am leaving fragments of my body in every dusty corner of this country and I have the scars to prove it.

Give me ten dollars, and I will show you everything.

THE FAMILY BUSINESS

Jackie's been here for twenty-five years and he tells me: *you get used to it.* He says your nose learns to seal itself when you dive headfirst into an ocean of dust; your eyes develop nictitating membranes to keep the chemical sprays out; and your hands... they will grow their own gloves, invisible and tough and permanent.

I've been a janitor for three weeks and I thought I was made of stronger materials.

We play chess in the breakroom. Jackie asks me what my favorite piece is. I say the pawn because, you know, he's the underdog; the odds are against him. Jackie identifies with the pawns too, but he sees nobility in their sacrifice; he sees beauty in their simplicity, in the fact that they're always moving forward.

Jackie shambles from room to room, moving half as fast as me but somehow getting twice as much done. The night shift will mess with your head like that. Jackie smiles, the saddest face I've ever seen.

Sometimes, I see that face and imagine that we are the servants entombed alive with the pharaoh, polishing someone else's gold while our oxygen runs out, dutifully preparing a grand feast for a god who will never be hungry.

But Jackie tells me that there is honor in this. *A good day's work. An honest living.* That there is poetry in this.

But what kind of poetry lives in a can of orange naturalizer, the liquid breath of dragons? The mist dissolves every word creeping up my throat, overwhelms every idea.

They got me wiping my reflection from the glass, scrubbing the shadows off the walls. They got me so scared of my alarm clock that I can't fall asleep any more, even when my muscles drain out from under my fingernails, my thoughts stream out of my ears, and I am left with nothing but two eyes that refuse to close for fear of what they might see. Is there really honor in this?

Or is that abstract notion the carrot they dangle in front of us pawns to move us across the board?

Jackie tells me you can't think about it like that. He says that without us, the people who live and work in this building couldn't function, that we keep the gears turning, and that it might not be glamorous, but it's necessary.

And of course: he's right. And maybe I am just a working class kid who somehow hustled my way into college and got delusions of grandeur. Maybe now I'm "too good" to go into the family business: a hundred generations of janitors and farmers and infantry and factory workers and pawns.

So I suck it up... and last for two more months. And on my final day, before a very uncertain future, I make a point to shake Jackie's hand, and I say:

> I've been thinking, man. I think the reason pawns can't move backwards is because if they could, they'd kill their own kings in a heartbeat.

> Instead, we are forced to keep moving, believing we can get to the other side and become royalty ourselves, but most likely dying on the way there, sacrificed for a cause we don't even understand. I wish you... I wish you the best, man. I wish you horses and castles.

Jackie smiles, the saddest face I've ever seen, and disappears into his work.

STARFISH

I am standing in a school, or a submarine. Everything is grey and the walls can almost kiss each other. Children avalanche around my legs, flowing into one another, their faces erased by their sheer numbers. It is too dark here. And my job, these days, is to turn all the lights on, and pretend to be brave.

We smell like unused paintbrushes; the air is still, hanging just over this river of hands and shoes and teeth. I see a teacher in a window, a smiley-face painted onto a crash-test dummy. I forget where I am going.

These children will grow up to be scarecrows. These children will snarl, once, at the world, and be put down. They will grow into the poems written about them, live in the spaces between the letters, and shiver when the books open.

And my job, these days, is to melt the winter with a flashlight.

I work in after-school program purgatory, moving from school to school, siphoning tears and collecting poems. I keep the poems in a shiny leather briefcase. I dump the tears out in the parking lot. And my job, these days, is to identify bodies. My job, these days, is to be the Disney World full-body-suit Sisyphus.

My job, these days, is to dream of starfish: tens of thousands smothered by the air on the beach, being pulled apart alive by the seagulls. I toss a few back into the ocean and people tell me that I'm making a difference.

But there is no honor in triage, only necessity.

And these children need something more, something bigger than one more plucky white woman to pry them open and extract their genius, or one more straight-A Teach for America mirage trying to "save" them, or one more Positive Male Role Model teaching them how to write poetry. And my job these days is to be one more positive male role model teaching them how to write poetry, and it's killing me.

A teacher once told me that this is direct service—we make a difference, just not enough of one. We are the bricks in a haunted house, doing an admirable job keeping the ceiling from collapsing, but not able to remove the evil from the air.

And my job, these days, is to be a hack exorcist. My job, these days, is to be a superhero in a coma, a strip mall Santa Claus. My job, these days, is to blindly feel my way through the jagged corners of these schools and not bleed too much.

And suddenly I remember where I'm going: the guidance counselor, who is concerned that one of my students might be *unstable* because she wrote a poem about her pain, not knowing that pain and anguish are pretty much all that 15-year-olds write about... and that the stage is one of the only spaces they have to talk about it, ever.

On my way to the office, an impossibly small boy from one of my sessions cannonballs through the crowd, hits me in the shoulder and says... *thank you*. His name is Brian. He says thank you, and means it, and I am made whole.

Somewhere between *you're welcome* and *I'm sorry*. I'm stuck staring at banners: Attitude is Everything, No Child Left Behind, I Love My School. I'm stuck. And my job, these days, is not to "make a difference." It is to fight, with everything I have, for a world in which I don't have to.

My job, these days, is to try to find a way to be both brick and builder, to teach starfish to fly.

THE SPILL

They fell upon us softly: leaves rustling around land mines, a blade buried in wet soil. Starving for the essence of our love, they enveloped us—first a few haunted homes on the outskirts of town, then into the proud city itself, then spreading, like a spilled can of burgundy paint across the map, swallowing.

Appetites attached to talons, blue-white fangs in children's mouths. Wine always escapes its cup, one way or another. We should have seen it coming, but when they appeared, pale and shrieking on the horizon, the might of ten thousand years of cups and dishes and goblets shattered, and the spill drowned every dream ever dreamt.

But you.

I found you treading water regardless—as invincible as canned food and two-by-fours. I found you exploding, brimstone on yours lips, tattooed with a fury as warm as the sun used to be. I found you beautiful: shaved head, Kevlar, bare hands. You cut them down. You broke them. You found knives between your knuckles and war clubs inside your leg bones.

I still remember how the ghost of a smile flickered across your eyes when you leaned in close and whispered to me:

Take the shotgun. I want the fireman's axe. I want to feel it. I want to feel them beneath it.

I knew then that I wanted to be with you for whatever forever we had left. Knew that we were to share an ancient love, a love bonded with flint and bone, that our skulls now carried within them a shining new darkness.

Our first date: fireballing through hordes of the undead: dull silver eyes, ragged hands reaching, screams bisected. Every gunshot a kiss, every swing of that axe a bedroom's liquid whisper. In this blackness I smelled your humanity, and aimed in the opposite direction.

Love, warm and grasping, splashed against the walls; love splashed onto our bodies; love splashing inside of us defiantly. And I found you in this smoking chaos; our shoulder blades kissed.

There may come a day when the sun bursts from the spider's belly to smile upon this world again. There may come a day when love can be represented by poetry, and romantic comedies, and candlelight dinners again; when it can be held, soft and round, in the palm of a child's hand.

But it is not on us to build that world. It is not on us to survive this one. Ours is not a love song sprouted from redemption, hope or even longing.

But it is a love song.

Sing it under your breath.

Sharpen it every morning.

If you should fall, I swear I'll come for you: two barrels erupting as one, an aluminum baseball bat strapped to my back, a pocketful of hand grenades, singing, pins already pulled.

TEN RESPONSES TO THE PHRASE "MAN UP"

1. Fuck you.

2. If you want to question my masculinity, like a schoolyard circle of curses, like a swordfight with lightsaber erections, save your breath.

Because contrary to what you may believe, not every problem can be solved by "growing a pair." You cannot arm-wrestle your way out of chemical depression. The CEO of the company that just laid you off does not care how much you bench. And I promise, there is no light beer in the universe full-bodied enough to make you love yourself.

3. Man up? Oh, that's that new superhero, right? Mild-mannered supplement salesman Mark Manstrong says the magic words *Man Up*, and then transforms into The Five O'Clock Shadow, the massively-muscled, deep-voiced, leather-duster-wearing superman who defends the world from, I don't know, feelings.

4. Of course. Why fight to remove our chains, when we can simply compare their lengths? Why step outside the box when the box has these badass flame decals on it? We men are cigarettes: dangerous... and poisonous.

5. You ever notice how nobody ever says *woman up*? They just imply it. Because women, and the women's movement, figured out a long time ago that being explicitly ordered around by commercials, magazines, and music is dehumanizing. When will men figure that out?

6. The phrase *man up* suggests that competence and perseverance are uniquely masculine traits. That women—not to mention any man who doesn't eat steak, drive a big pickup truck and have lots of sex (with women)—are nothing more than background characters, comic relief, props.

More than anything, though, it suggests that to be yourself— whether you wear skinny jeans, rock a little eyeliner, drink some other brand of light beer, or write poetry—will cost you.

7. How many boys have to kill themselves before this country acknowledges the problem? How many women have to be assaulted? How many trans people have to be murdered?

We teach boys how to wear the skin of a man, but we also teach them how to raise that skin like a flag and draw blood for it.

8. Boy babies get blue socks. Girl babies get pink socks. What about purple? What about orange, yellow, chartreuse, cerulean, black, tie-dyed, buffalo plaid, rainbow?

9. I want to be free to express myself. *Man up.* I want to have meaningful, emotional relationships with my brothers. *Man up.* I want to be weak sometimes. *Man up.* I want to be strong in a way that isn't about physical power or dominance. *Man up.* I want to talk to my son about something other than sports. *Man up.* I want to ask for help. *Man up.* I want to be who I am. *Man up.*

10. No.

HANDSHAKES

The weirdest thing about having your hand crushed is that the pair of eyes across from yours never stops smiling. As knuckles are compressed, as the skin is all but torn off the top of your hand, he always has this grin on his face. Even as the vein bulges from his neck, he smiles, until you grudgingly mumble, *that's quite a handshake*, and he releases you.

As a young man, I was taught that one's masculinity is tied directly to one's handshake, that when meeting another man for the first time, no sin was more unforgivable than placing a limp fish in his hand, the dead husk of a greeting. Your grip must be firm, like the way you hold your briefcase as you walk to work, or the way you hold the handle while standing up on the bus.

Some men, however, prefer a grip like a battle-axe mid swing, like ripping the head off an antelope by tugging on the antlers. Some men treat every handshake like a gladiator's death-match, a test of strength, a test of will.

And when I meet these men, as I often do, their tectonic plate handshakes never fail to illuminate my myriad perceived inadequacies. Frozen there with purple fingertips, I am reminded that I cannot stand the taste of beer, that cars confuse and frighten me, that when faced with a barbeque and a pair of tongs, I will overcook the meat every time. These men attempt to squeeze the testosterone from my body.

Maybe I'm just insecure. But studying his smirk more closely, I think maybe that would make two of us. Because as he wrings the color from my fingers I find myself wanting to ask him:

Do you ever feel trapped? In the mornings, when you're watching TV and happily downing that protein shake made from raw eggs, liquefied steak and Axe Body Spray, do you ever crush the glass between your fingers?

Do you ever get tired of that voice in the back your head, you know, the one that sounds just like Dennis Leary, telling you to constantly reaffirm that you're a "real man" by catcalling women, eating enormous hamburgers, getting into physical altercations over trivial bullshit, and squeezing everything really, really hard?

I find myself wanting to ask him: Do you hold your wife's arm like this when you're angry with her?

Is there a teddy bear, somewhere in your history, being ripped away from a pair of hands that just aren't *strong* enough? Do you remember the first time your father wouldn't let you hold his hand when crossing the street? Do you remember the way he looked at you? Do you remember being handed your first-born son and not knowing how to hold him? Do you remember squeezing his shoulders like this the first time he disappointed you?

Do you remember what it was you were trying to hold on to?

And I know: there is so much space between us, as men, that sometimes we feel compelled to cram as much contact as we physically can into every touch. I know.

We've become so comfortable with crushing, so hypnotized by our own strength, we forget: how incredible it can feel to let go.

ACTION

There is a conversation that never happened. Not even a deleted scene; more like a storyboard lost, an idea cut from the first draft. You are co-starring, slouched on the futon while we watch the game, telling me about your new girlfriend. Or more specifically, telling me about all the things you're going to do to your new girlfriend. Action.

And part of me still remembers my lines, even though I never said them. The conversation I just couldn't start, for fear of... what? Awkwardness? Or hurting our friendship? Or simply because the commercials were over? That one tiny gesture that might not have changed anything, but might have. I remember, how I never muted the TV, never put my drink down, and never said:

Man—the way you talk about her, the way you treat her... Your hands are getting too big for your heart. I can smell the future you on your breath. She isn't safe with you.

And now it's two weeks later and we're standing in my kitchen, that same silence between us. She didn't want to press charges, so you are a convict with sledgehammer hands and no boulders to break them on. And I am thinking about how we used to play football together. Numbers 55 and 56, both inside linebackers. I am remembering the dozens of conversations that never happened, the words oversleeping in the bed of my lungs. I am the least important person in this story.

And part of me wants to believe that you wouldn't have listened anyway, that some evil spirit whispered itself into your skull. Part of me wants to believe that we didn't grow up three blocks from each other, that our eyes aren't the same color. Part of me is always repeating those lines, always shooting that scene, always reminding myself that despite this guilt, I'm not a bad guy.

You tell me that she never said no. That you're sorry. That you're not a bad guy.

Rape culture is silence. It is being able to see the future and not doing anything about it. It is believing the fairy tale platitude that there are good people and bad people and that as long as you're not one of the bad people, your job is done, your conscience is clear.

It is all of us swimming through the same polluted water of beer commercials policing masculinity, stand-up comedians making rape jokes to sound "edgy," media talking heads blaming the victim, music turning women into objects, language encouraging us to think of sex *as* violence—*bang, hit, smash.*

It is telling our daughters to dress sensibly and not walk alone at night, and telling our sons...

It is a conversation that never happened. And this is not an excuse for you—it is a reminder for me.

That while her silence will always mean *no*; my silence, this silence between us, will always mean *yes.*

CONSENT AT 10,000 FEET

You ever have sex in a haunted house? Like you know, you sneak in together, and you're both laughing, and you got it all planned out because you both worked there last year and know the layout of the building, and then, like, a werewolf jumps out and it's like *aaahhh!* but then you find that one spare room and it's like... *aahhh...* you know: it's different, it's outside the box, but there's nothing *wrong* with it.

You ever go to your roommate's fringe festival show and end up hooking up with one of the supporting cast members, but they're like, a method actor in the middle of a series of performances, so they never break character? And it's cool, but their character is this, like, alternate universe steampunk Mercutio and their blunderbuss keeps getting in the way, and you both laugh about it, and it's memorable, something beyond the norm, but there's nothing *wrong* with it.

You ever have sex inside an enormous bowl of fettuccine alfredo that is suspended by chains between two sequoia trees because you're dating this super avant garde performance artist and wanted to draw attention to their new vanity publishing press but you only got like a hundred Twitter followers? Yeah, it's squishy, and definitely an experience that is not easily replicated, but there is nothing *wrong* with it.

There is nothing *wrong* with any of these scenarios, because in all of them, both partners are 100%, flamboyantly beyond any shadow of a doubt, *down* with what's happening; and the communication of that, verbal and nonverbal, is clear and constant. This is consent. And wrong... would be the absence of that. In any context. For any reason.

It would be silence. It would be *I don't know if this is what I want right now*. Because maybe that's not a no, but it's definitely not a yes. It would be just about everyone agreeing that rape is bad, but only when it's called *rape*; how the amount of people who will admit to getting someone drunk, or otherwise manipulating, coercing, or forcing them into a sexual act is so much larger than the amount who will admit to raping someone.

How wrong is it, to continue to talk about sexual assault like it's always that stranger lurking in the bushes, or always that cartoon caricature of a predatory fratboy and never... the boyfriend. Or the girlfriend. Or the best friend. Or the "ally." Or that really sweet guy from class.

This is for that really sweet guy from class, who might be asking: *what about the grey areas? What if we're just both really drunk? What if she sends mixed messages? What if I'm trying to do the right thing but I read those signals wrong?*

Have you ever had sex while skydiving? Like where you talk about consent the same way you talk about wearing a parachute—no grey areas, no assumptions like, *I'm pretty sure I'm wearing a parachute*. No questions like, *I asked her to check my parachute and she didn't say anything, but it was okay last time so I'm sure it's good this time too.*

Have you ever had sex in a burning building, when smoke and cinder wrapped itself around your neck, but coming was more important to you than going? Have you ever had sex on a life raft in the middle of the ocean, surrounded by sharks? I'm not saying the water can't be cloudy. I'm just saying: we are under no obligation to swim through it.

Have you ever not had sex? Just watched a movie, maybe made out, maybe made plans to go out again later, and then maybe days or weeks later, when you're both there, and both ready, and both smiling, and both completely alive in your own bodies, and both listening to each other, fully; and maybe it isn't love, maybe it's just sex, and that's perfectly okay, but "love" is so much bigger than *let's spend our lives together*; it is also *let's spend this moment together* as two (or more) people: present, electric, the opposite of grey, the embodiment of human: hands, eyes, lips, everything.

FIVE THINGS MEN CAN DO TO DISRUPT AND DISMANTLE RAPE CULTURE

I wrote this on the airplane to a college gig where I wanted to be able to present something practical and actionable to go along with the previous two poems. I thought a lot about whether to include it in this collection, because it's really just a rough, conversational version of the kind of bullet-pointed "ally thinkpiece" that a lot of people have already written, especially online. In workshops and educational spaces, I generally defer to those voices instead, and/or have a dialogue with the audience to organically build a list like this. But since I did write this, I figured I'd err on the side of transparency and include it here.

I'm a poet, but this is not a poem. It'll be structured like one, and I will perform it like one, but it's not really a poem. Because while there is tremendous power in poetry, in storytelling, and in putting a human face on an issue, there is *also* power, sometimes, in just saying what the hell you want to say, as simply and straightforwardly as possible. So what follows are five things men can do to disrupt and dismantle rape culture.

Because while this work is everyone's work, including women and gender-nonconforming people, men occupy specific spaces in our society and should be thinking critically about how those spaces might be transformed. Also, because I am a cisgender man, this list is as much for me as it is for anyone who happens to be listening.

1. Listen. AKA shut up and listen
When women talk about the prevalence of street harassment and catcalling, about embedded sexism in the workplace, about real-life experiences of rape and sexual violence, and the lack of support and resources for survivors, remember: you do not have to "chime in." You do not have to lighten the mood by making a joke, or offering an alternate interpretation of what she experienced. Nobody wants to hear you play "devil's advocate."

Speaking up is important. Shutting up is also important. And as men, we could do a much better job of just shutting up and listening sometimes. Shutting up and listening, however, is not enough.

2. Strive to be more thoughtful and informed

If you're one of those guys who hears the phrase "rape culture" and interprets it as "all men are evil and all women are victims and you're a bad person and I hate you!" ...you don't know what rape culture means.

So learn. And that doesn't mean relying on women to teach you, or take time out of their lives to explain every bullet point to you. Take the initiative. Read books. Read articles. Take classes. Google terms like "enthusiastic consent." The info is all out there.

And even apart from just being more informed, we can challenge ourselves to think and act in more thoughtful, intentional ways. We can be more mindful of the language we use. We can check ourselves. But again, being a more thoughtful and informed individual is not enough.

3. On an interpersonal level, we can serve as forces of disruption

When we hear a joke that trivializes rape, we can speak up about it. When we see a Facebook comment that amounts to *she was asking for it*, we can say something. When we witness catcalling on the bus, we can do something—maybe it's standing up and saying *hey dude that's not cool*, or maybe it's as simple as just distracting the guy, asking what time it is, asking for directions, etc. When we're at a party, we can look out for each other—not just as men, but as human beings.

(We can also consider these actions while also considering the various identities that we hold and our own safety and potential effectiveness in a given context—it's about intentionality.)

We can cultivate awareness, and just pay attention to what's going on. Maybe that means drinking less sometimes. Maybe that means interrupting a situation where someone may not be able to make conscious, intentional choices. We can do something. But again, disrupting harmful behaviors when we see them is not enough.

4. We can be proactive and disrupt harmful behaviors before they happen

Let's be proactive about bringing these conversations into spaces that aren't just women's studies classes, poetry slams and Twitter. How much power does a football coach have when he talks about consent with his players? How far can this message go when it's being spread by rappers, CEOs, labor activists, the organizers of comic book conventions, online forum mods, best friends, and fathers?

And again, disrupting harmful behaviors, even when done in a proactive way, is not enough.

5. Organize

Because yes, we need to learn more, we need to have more conversations and we need to challenge ourselves and the people around us to do better. But really disrupting rape culture, and ultimately dismantling it, is going to take fundamental shifts not just in our attitudes, but in our policies, laws and institutions too.

And this will look different in different communities. Maybe it's about joining an organization like PAVE (Promoting Awareness, Victim Empowerment) or Men Can Stop Rape, or starting a similar one. Maybe it's about engaging in a campaign to found and fund a rape crisis center in your neighborhood. Maybe it's about volunteering as an advocate and going through a training program so you can not only do some good work, but be better positioned to create bigger-picture change as well. Maybe it's about educating yourself about the issue of sexual assault in prisons, in the armed forces, or on college campuses, and then meeting up with like-minded people and building some kind of sustainable, long-term solution.

And no, organizing isn't enough either. No single point on this list is enough.

What is enough, though, is us. Changing a culture is not the same as changing one person's behavior. It takes a steady push, a collective effort: radicals and moderates, the privileged and the oppressed, people of all gender identities, plugging in how and when and where we can, fighting for something better.

As many have been saying for a long time now—there are no allies, only actions. What we believe matters, but only as far as it impacts what we do.

And the good news here is that we can do something. We must do something. And we will do something.

MICKEY MOUSE GAS MASK

When my grandma was little, growing
up in Hawai'i during the War, she had her
eyes on a Mickey Mouse Gas Mask.

All the kids got masks: a line like any
other. Waiting, walking, waiting again.
But since *Yatogo* falls

at the end of the alphabet, by the time
it was her turn, all the Mickey Mouse
Gas Masks were taken.

I've never had to pick out a gas mask.
But growing up in Wisconsin, not during
a war, Mickey Mouse was everywhere,

smiling. He'd try to peek in our windows, or hide
around corners, but one ear would always stick out,
a reminder, a spirit, a tradition, a threat.

QUICKSAND

Upon stumbling, by chance, upon a man, waist-deep in quicksand, I need a second to process. After all: quicksand? This is fiction made flesh; it's like going to the zoo and seeing a mermaid. So my first response, naturally, is to tell him:

Hey, um, I'm pretty sure that I read somewhere that quicksand isn't actually dangerous, that this idea of a patch of sandy water sucking a person down into oblivion is just a tall tale, a trope to build tension in early 1960s westerns. In real life, yeah, I mean, a person could hypothetically get caught in quicksand, but it's not very common and not really that hard to get out. So are you sure you're sinking in quicksand?

He sinks.

My words don't seem to have any effect. So being an open-minded, progressive individual, I reevaluate. Maybe quicksand is real. So what now? My second response upon stumbling, by chance, upon a man, chest deep in quicksand, is, before I actually *do* anything, to make sure that I have the *whole* picture. I mean, what was this guy doing out here in the jungle all alone? Did he step into that quicksand on purpose? Was he kind of asking for it? Does he have a criminal record? Maybe I should wait until all the facts come in.

He sinks.

And again, being an open-minded, progressive individual, I decide to give him the benefit of the doubt, at least for now. I want to help.

So my third response upon stumbling, by chance, upon a man, neck deep in quicksand, is, obviously, to recite a poem. To throw some spirit energy his way. To describe, out loud, just how heavy my heart is. I take a piece of paper out of my backpack, and with a pen, I write *quicksand is bad and I am an* ally *to people who fall in it.* I pin that piece of paper to my chest. I take out my phone and I tweet: *when are we going to wake up? #quicksand.*

He sinks.

And being an open-minded, progressive individual, I decide that this isn't enough; that we, as a society, need to address the root causes of people sinking in quicksand. So my fourth response upon stumbling, by chance, upon a man, forehead-deep in quicksand, is to take a moment and really acknowledge, and think about, my privilege as someone who is not sinking in quicksand. I vow to... take a class, to challenge my friends when they make quicksand-related jokes, to be more mindful of how I navigate the world.

He sinks.

And being an open-minded, progressive individual, I decide that the time for words has passed; now is the time for action. So my fifth response upon stumbling, by chance, upon a man, disappeared into quicksand, is... is...

We can't allow ourselves to forget what happened here. I know that we need to *do* something, to put up a sign, to educate people, to build a bridge over this patch of quicksand. I just don't have any wood. I just have this boundless font of paper and pens and rope, what can one person do?

I imagine my lungs filling with mud. Black earth. Brown water. The hike back to my hotel will be full of reflection. I say a prayer under my breath. It is the least I can do.

A FRAMEWORK FOR HOW I THINK ABOUT SOCIAL MEDIA SUPPORTING SOCIAL MOVEMENTS

"Quicksand" is the kind of poem that I always try to make sure to have a discussion around after performing. I think it's easy to misinterpret. So this brief essay is a kind of extension of the thought process in that poem. It was also written during the 2015 Baltimore Uprising in response to the death of Freddie Gray, and the online version includes a number of links to other resources.

When we become aware of an injustice, especially as people who are not directly impacted by that injustice, I believe that there is a spectrum of responses. It is not just that some responses are bad and others are good, (although, to be sure, some *are* bad or good); it's that it can become important to acknowledge that some actions are both *good* and *not enough*, and that we can recognize that without devaluing the action itself.

Looking at social media practices as a microcosm of larger social processes, I'm trying to get at a more nuanced way to think about how we can respond to injustice.

I'd like to be clear that this framework is what I try to remind *myself* of, not how I think all people everywhere need to operate. If other people can relate to this or use it, great, but I'm not trying to dictate anything to anyone. Especially when I think about my own identities and positionality, these points only really make sense in that context. For example, telling a Black person "you should do more to educate people about racism" would be a super messed-up thing to say. But telling myself that would not be. So please read this spectrum with that in mind.

Also, I'm not particularly interested in being "deep" here. This isn't some profound philosophical discussion about how human beings relate to change-making processes, or a poetic exploration of the roots of racial violence; it's a concrete look at how social media practice can relate to movement-building, especially in the context of the #BaltimoreUprising and #FreddieGray protests.

First, imagine a spectrum; the first point here is at one extreme, and the others create a line toward the opposite end.

|---|

1. **Silence:** Some people are silent because they're ignorant, or because they don't care, but there's also a case to be made, especially for white people, that silence can mean listening, or trying to not take up space: two good impulses. But as the rest of this list shows, there are ways to speak up without speaking over others, especially when we're talking about social media practice. There's just too much at stake to be completely silent.

2. **Platitudes:** "We all just need to LOVE each other!" Some platitudes are innocent, but a good amount of them implicitly amount to "why are you talking about this? I'd prefer to not think about it." See also: #AllLivesMatter, which means nothing, leads to no meaningful action, and only serves to derail the important conversation that #BlackLivesMatter is initiating.

3. **"Thoughts and prayers:"** The last thing I want to do is disrespect people who are authentically trying to process tragedy and injustice. But I struggle with this one. If saying "my thoughts and prayers are with Baltimore" helps you survive, then I support that; this spectrum, after all, applies to me and yours might look different. But for me, I don't give my own thoughts or prayers much weight. Sometimes a phrase like this can be an excuse to disengage, to say something when you feel powerless to do anything. But I don't believe in powerlessness, as the following points illustrate.

4. Outrage: Sometimes, this is just raw emotion, and that's fine. "This country is messed up and we need to do something" is a great sentiment, and one I agree with. But this point is in the middle of the spectrum for a reason.

5. Outrage + links to more information: Social media can be really powerful, but not just for the vague push-and-pull of culture battles. It can be used to legitimately transmit information that can be used for the building of movements. So saying "this country is messed up and we need to do something" *and* linking to an article that provides background information, on-the-ground reporting, and/or useful analysis, can be a step in a helpful direction.

6. Outrage + links to concrete actions or organizations: When the question "but what can I do?" is on so many people's minds, I return to the idea that systemic problems require solutions that are bigger than just "striving to be a better person." That means organizing: joining and/or supporting activist organizations that are doing the work. Of course, no organization is perfect, and no single event can magically "fix" things. But these are vital first steps. Social media is a great tool for transmitting when and where rallies, educational events, city council meetings, organizational meetings, and other plug-in points are happening.

7. Signal-boosting the activists on the ground: I don't always do this, since it can be tempting to center my social media practice on my own thoughts and opinions. But I think the "tweet less, retweet more" impulse is important. I have opinions, but I'm not in Baltimore, or Ferguson; beyond that, I'm also not Black, and this movement is very much about how #BlackLivesMatter. So shout out to people like @osope, @aliciagarza, @opalayo, @deray, @prisonculture, @karnythia, @blacklivesmpls, @nvlevy, @micamaryjane, @eveewing, @blklivesmatter, @dreamdefenders, @wintanamn, and the hundreds of other activists and organizers out there.

Keeping this spectrum in mind has helped me sharpen my social media practice; I hope it can be useful to others as well.

AN OPEN LETTER TO PINOCCHIO FROM DRACULA

Let me tell you about flesh. We danced in their living
rooms while they slept, squeezed through keyholes and

soundlessly caressed the insides of their loved ones. Glory:
pillowcases painted dawn, pulling real boys out from

under our fingernails. No, flesh is not your wish. More
likely normalcy, the electricity of a lover, the chill of

dusk, the ability to smell. *Remember—the creatures
of the night belong to me, including the crickets. They talk.*

Your wish: for flesh bubbling around your walnut heart,
for blood cascading through your wooden joints; more

likely the wish of a leaf to drop and join its brothers
on the forest floor, a tortured prisoner biting off his own

tongue to choke. *Remember: that spirit inside you is not
yours. You only feed it.* We are more than the materials

with which we have been built. Paint your skin, ratchet
the angle of your spine, but keep this magic burning—

too much leaked away already, like the skin peeling
off a snake, like an angel starving to death, like the last

music ever. *Remember: abomination is just another word
for miracle.* Half-extinct, we are still gods; let us pray.

HOW TO EXPLAIN WHITE SUPREMACY TO A
WHITE SUPREMACIST

Sometimes, you are a lit match dropped into a boiling ocean. Sometimes, you are a stray dog proud of the sunrise after a long night of barking at the moon. Sometimes, you scream at the television, shadowbox mushroom clouds; your hand-to-hand hatred outclassed, outdated. You: post-apocalyptic litterbug. You: venomous spider in the basement of a burning building. You: whose anger is so vast, and so empty—all teeth, and no mouth, just that white rattle.

Remember: white supremacy is not a shark; it is the water. It is how we talk about *racism* as white hoods and confederate flags, knowing that you own those things, and we don't... as if we didn't own this history too, this system—we tread water.

And you: chum in a bucket. How many skinheads do you think are in the room when they set immigration law? Or decide curriculum for public schools? Or push policies like redlining, mandatory minimum sentencing, benign neglect, gentrification, broken windows policing, voter ID, stop and frisk, three strikes, the drug war? Remember: the eye of the hurricane is the least destructive part.

You: meanest glare in the chatroom, all poker-face and no cards. Was it your politically incorrect YouTube comment that made the median net worth of Black families in this country nine percent the median net worth of white families?

Which individual Donald Trump bigot bogeyman are we supposed to be angry at about the millions of people impacted by discrimination in housing, and banking, and education, and employment, and the criminal justice system, each year? Remember: sharks kill about one person each year; thousands drown.

So, when there is a new name hashtagged each week, when police create more Black stars than Hollywood; how long do we keep pointing out the bad apples, ignoring the fact that the orchard was planted on a mass grave? ...and that *we* planted it there?

Because of course, this isn't really a poem for white supremacists. I don't know any white supremacists.

But I know a lot of people in this room. And I know myself. And I know how white supremacy is upheld, whether through our action, our inaction, or just through paying our tuition and taxes. How it isn't just the broken treaty; it is also the treaty. How a gavel can speak as loudly as a grenade. How a white fratboy in blackface on Halloween and his friend, who knows it's wrong but doesn't say anything, begin to blur together.

How the real racists, today, are so often not even racist. Those teeth, sharper when smiling, sharper still when smiling and meaning it.

A burning cross is so dramatic. Just say: *I don't see race.* Just say: *we all have an equal chance if we work hard.* Just say: *all lives matter.* Just say nothing; surround yourself with others who say nothing, and convince yourself that silence is the only song: this muted, underwater melody, this pulsing quiet.

And when a chorus blooms in Baltimore, when trumpets sound in Ferguson, when every one of our cities breaks... into song, will we hear it? Will we choose to listen? Or will we just continue treading water, watching for that great, white, shark... not realizing that we're drowning?

CONFESSIONS OF A WHITE RAPPER

A pocketful of props, a quick pound and a handshake
A free mixtape, a highway through a landscape
as far from the Bronx as heaven is
A moment of uncertainty, moment of clarity, moment of hesitance
A bio with a spark of truth,
a couple sharpies, Party Music and The Carter Two
Labcabincalifornia, Illmatic and Headshots,
A couple handbills left in the back of a reststop,
A rhymebook, a sticker with my name on it
stickin' through the rain washin' all the other flyers down;
hoodie up, fitted to the side, bottled water, last minute to decide
setlists, rep this: livin' for the rhyme
but moreso for what that rhyme represents:
forty-five minutes of our lives to connect
Broken hearts over breakbeats, live and direct
from the belly of the beast, strivin' to get free...

Confessions of a white rapper:

1. KRS-ONE says there are nine elements of hip hop, a solar system of art, and fashion, and innovation, orbiting an inferno. Some promoters will book me over a Black MC because they don't want to attract *the wrong element.*

2. It is easier for me to get a buzz going because most bloggers, radio DJs, publicists, music journalists, videographers and booking agents are white. And I don't even really identify as a white rapper; I'm mixed. But *that* usually doesn't fit on the flyer.

3. Listeners, who are often white, and identify with me because of it, actively seek out meaning in my music, rather than just looking for a good beat to dance to. And I will readily admit: I am very talented. But is that talent the reason you bought my album, the reason you came to my show, the reason you want this interview? I will never know.

4. I can code-switch on a dime. We developed warp technology years ago and will leave this solar system as soon as we find a more fashionable one.

5. My music can be perceived as rebellious because it's hip hop, but safe because of my skin. Fans and listeners get to engage with an oppositional culture without ever leaving their racialized comfort zones. Tarzan is the king of the jungle. Tom Cruise is the last samurai. Michael J. Fox goes back in time and invents rock and roll in 1955.

6. The thing about stealing is that it's addictive. A little here. A little more. And we all know it's not wrong to steal to feed your starving family... and white kids in America are hungry.

Whose food are they eating? Whose food are you eating? Whose food am I eating?

7. Maybe white people don't belong in hip hop. But white people don't really belong in America, when you think about it. So we are left with questions. Like, what is the difference between acknowledging your privilege and acting on that acknowledgment? How do we move forward? How do we define progress? Who is we? Who should be we? Who deserves to belong in the category *we*?

8. When I say *one small step for man,* you say *one giant leap for mankind.* Just remember whose planet you're standing on.

9. The code of the white rapper is this: know the history, build community, put people on. And if they ever make you a monument, scratch your name out. Break it. Spit on it. Burn it.

We are not tourists, but we are also not the native inhabitants of this land. Aliens. Invaders. Put your hands up. Put your fucking hands up.

THE INVISIBLE BACKPACKER OF PRIVILEGE

(from the album "You Better Weaponize")

Guante:
I don't identify as white, but I identify as white enough
to get that indie rap writer buzz,
and benefit from a system set up
for rappers who already have advantages to get love
Think about it: how many music writers are white?
How many bloggers, how many booking agents?
How many college radio DJs?
How many publicists, concert-goers and critics got white faces?
'Cause you can watch 8 mile and assume
white rappers got it hard, but it isn't really true
This is America; even if you're not racist,
racism's in the foundation, face it
I'm not saying white people can't participate,
(obviously) I'm just saying please eliminate
the myth that it's just about hard work and lyrical ability
'cause it's about responsibility
Know the history, put people on, build community
'cause not everyone who works hard earns it
And if they ever make you a monument,
scratch your name out, break it, spit on it, burn it
Yo, it's so messed up how
you talk about whiteness and half your fanbase shuts down
So nod your head, you ain't got to understand us
Just put your hands up, put your fucking hands up

Chantz Erolin:
Ayo white kid, yeah, yeah, I hate to say it like this
but I'm trying to help you get enlightened to having light skin
Don't trip, I don't hate kids, and someone's gonna call me racist
but I'm running out of patience, so I gotta say this

I know it's hard for you to see or conceive, what it means to be me
Well, not me, but be defined by what society sees
They say I'm to believe
we're "post racial" but still, I feel confined by police
This dude called the cops on my crib the other night,
saying that I robbed his wife, or well some dude that wasn't white
Maybe Native, maybe Asian;
either way, three squad cars hit my crib at 3 AM
And no white boy, in no way is that your fault
You may hate pigs and think that profiling is awful
But understand that you would not be in that position
just for smoking on your porch with your particular pigment
You got the privilege of not having to deal with your race,
while my relatives are off putting bleach on their face
I used to wish I was white, but I'm disgusted by skin creams
I was bullied and cryin' without knowing what "chink" means
Have severe doubts you'll be bumping this song
or humming along
You've been taught that skin color means nothing at all,
and whiteness is considered normal and neutral
You may not notice race when them white rappers do shows
It's crazy in a rap show devoid of brown and Black folk,
hearing white kids saying words they should get smacked for
This shit was built on the backs of our oppression
Now you think it's just your raps that leave impressions?
Hands up

RP Hooks:
Foolish with no glory, tap dancing, drinking 40's
Don't judge me if you do not know my story
And I'll do the same, it's more than just a name, nigga
Mainframe spinning like I'm Twista knowing
most of these listeners won't understand
Race and change; I guess it's time to grow up
If you can't acknowledge how you got here, don't even show up
The token Black leaving heart attacks

more righteous than my phonies speaking stories of my homies
on some things they never knew, they only heard about
Darker than the couch up in my mama's house
My roots are deeper than these double standards
so I'm speaking out: Love it when we're all connected in the 'sota,
but I can't respect my brother if he can't respect my culture
Moving fast like Testarossa growing up: dream in color, kid
I'm in living color, on my Wayans brothers spit
Hoping that my whiter color brother can relate to this
If he can't, we can change how bad our separation gets
Preaching on the newest testament like we're in Nazareth
Press they love me 'cause I'm cosigned by my lighter publicist
Knowing that we're all connected, to police I plead the fifth
No equality in this, if you racist or you hate this
you can give my ass a kiss; please no lipstick on your lips
'cause I don't want to change my color, not even a little bit
In the end, all I ask is you acknowledge privilege
Cause I promise you, you wouldn't be poppin' in '96

ON RACISM, PRIVILEGE AND HIP HOP

The last two pieces show how writing a spoken word poem and writing a rap song require different approaches. The two don't so much complement one another as they simply coexist as two different variations on the same subject; they even share some lines. This kind of cannibalization and cross-pollination has been an important element of my work, because acknowledging context/audience is important.

"The Invisible Backpacker of Privilege" features me, Chantz Erolin and RP Hooks talking about how whiteness functions in indie hip hop and beyond, exploring concepts of appropriation, privilege and responsibility.

The title of the song is a reference to Peggy McIntosh's "Unpacking the Invisible Knapsack of Privilege." The term "backpacker" is casual slang for underground hip hop fan.

Depending on the listener, I'd imagine, it's either extremely straightforward or quite frustrating and confusing, so I wanted to take this opportunity to dig a little more deeply into what the song is trying to say.

What Privilege Means
The concept of privilege isn't as complicated or controversial as its critics would have us believe. Basically, our identities impact how we move through the world and how people treat us; some identities (white, male, straight, rich, etc.) confer certain advantages, and/or are seen as either "normal" or desirable.

In the context of the song, it means that even though hip hop was borne out of and is still driven by Black musical tradition, whiteness (especially here in Minnesota) carries certain "perks" with it. This may include ease of networking (with white music writers, venue owners, DJs, bloggers, etc.), lack of negative stereotypes, more access to certain spaces (clubs, colleges, etc.), the capacity to potentially sell more CDs to fans who identify with you, the ability to make "edgy" music with a "safe" face on it— the list goes on.

Clearly, this is bigger than hip hop. This song is about using hip hop as a lens through which we can see how privilege functions everywhere. If white privilege exists in a rap scene, what about in a school, corporation, bank, the criminal justice system, government, or in a thousand other places?

What Privilege Does Not Mean
Privilege does not mean that "all white people have an easy life" or that "no rich person has ever worked hard" or that "no woman can ever be as successful." I feel like a lot of the pushback to privilege discourse comes from this kind of fundamental misunderstanding of what we're actually talking about.

So when I hear students say "but I'm white and I had to struggle; I don't feel privileged," I get it. That's a valid statement; it's just incomplete. Being oppressed in one identity (race, gender, class, sexual orientation, etc.) doesn't mean that you can't be privileged in another. They don't cancel each other out; they exist simultaneously. Privilege isn't always about a tangible advantage; sometimes it's about the *lack* of a specific set of disadvantages that you may not even be aware of.

This song is not saying that white rappers will always succeed and rappers of color will always fail; that's obviously not the case. But privilege isn't just about those "perks" that play out on an individual level; there will always be exceptions to those rules. The more important concept here is power. Privilege is also about general trends and patterns. It's about what gets propped up as "normal" or desirable and what gets stereotyped as dangerous or bad on a broader scale.

Even if there are many successful artists of color, we still have to look at who owns the labels, who profits from radio play/CD sales, who gets to create art on their own terms and who has to follow a format in order to pay their advance back. Even if rap bloggers trip over each other hyping up the most "authentic" MCs, we still have to interrogate why they do that—is it a genuine love for the culture, or is something else going on?

It's not just about the two dozen artists who make it to the top; hip hop is an ecosystem comprised of millions of people—artists, engineers, promoters, fans, etc.—and this song is about recognizing how privilege plays out at every level.

Especially here in Minnesota (admittedly, this song won't have the same relevance in every scene, though it will always have some), we need to do better. It's easy to have a "we're all just humans, dude" attitude when you refuse to see the persistent trends of who makes it vs. who doesn't, who gets media attention vs. who gets media support (not the same thing), and how that aforementioned hip hop ecosystem functions.

Again, I'm not saying that race is the deciding factor in all of those questions—just that it plays a role. To ignore that is dangerous.

"Acknowledging Privilege" is the First Step, Not the Last

One reason that I'm proud of this song is that I think the three of us did a good job tackling the issue in context; we know that a big part of our audience is actively resistant to this stuff, another big part has never thought about it before, and another big part has thought about it so much that they're ready to move beyond the privilege framework into more radical places.

Because it's not like no one's ever written songs about this before; Macklemore and Murs both come to mind. But this song is about digging deeper, about "next steps." So much social justice education focuses on intro'ing concepts of privilege and oppression, and that's not enough.

The question I ask in my verse is "what now?" We could have an academic argument about whether white people should be rapping, but the fact is that white people *are* rapping, so let's talk about what that means, and what responsibilities come with that.

"Know the history, build community, and put people on" are starting points, at least for me. That's the baseline. I hope we can continue to build from there. See you in the YouTube comments.

GHOST HUNTERS

[*a VHS cassette*]
Holy instrument, silver on black velvet.
The whine of static, Geiger counter clicking.
Sweat all over the flashlight, ready.
Check. Wires unwound, a greedy tangle.
Tiny red light like sunset. Check.
The tape is spinning. Check. Ready,
as the light screams back into the bottle.

[*a different VHS cassette*]
We caught one once in Syria, a white shirt
with a thousand sleeves dancing, a dust devil.
A local boy gave us his only bullet
to exorcise the thing. We sold it for petrol,
watched the thing in the rearview mirror,
bigger and bigger and bigger.

[*a different VHS cassette*]
It's not so much the ghosts as it is the hunting:
hours in old hallways, other people's bedrooms,
cold cellars, a lighthouse no one cares about.

[*a different VHS cassette*]
Stinky library pulp ghost gurgling
purple-black curses from inside the cage.
Another wrapped its wispy tendrils gently
around my wrist; it took a Gurkha blade to pry me loose.
Washed that night for hours before realizing
the water was another, a laughing maw.
So many now dragged into the rocks
and torn apart, burned, buried, digested. .
This houseboat would be haunted
were that remotely possible.

[*a different VHS cassette*]
My sweat is holy water;
not because I am religious,
because I drink so much of it.

CHERRY SPOON BRIDGE TO NOWHERE

1.

So, I'm an MC, and my stage name is *Guante*, and my last name is *Tran Myhre*, so at the end of every show, there's always one person who kind of awkwardly approaches me, like: *so... what are you?* And it's not an easy question to answer; it is a complicated and emotional topic. I'm mixed, both by blood and by history, but... if you saw a picture of me in a magazine, what would you see? A white guy. So there's always a kind of tension between my abstract heart and the more concrete reality of privilege, between internal and external identities.

And maybe that's why I feel so at home here, in the Twin Cities, a community inextricably bound to that tension. Where the arts and literary and musical scenes are all so diverse and vibrant and beautiful. But if you saw a picture of them in a magazine, what would you see? White people. This is not a question of diversity; it is a question of who *edits* this metaphorical magazine. Who funds it? Who profits from it?

Have you ever been in a magazine? Who decided that your story mattered, that your voice deserved an audience? Have you ever hung in a gallery? Have you ever bared your soul to the abyss only to have it chuckle back at you? When asked "what are you?" have you ever answered honestly.

2.

In a Facebook Q&A, The Ordway Theater's Artistic Director responded to 46 questions regarding the decision to produce Miss Saigon despite community outcry and protest of the musical's racist elements, by saying: *Miss Saigon is a complicated and emotional topic.* ...and nothing else.

It is one thing to chuckle at their callousness or cluelessness. It is something else to refuse to acknowledge that this is how just about every arts and media institution operates, every day. When they say *our programs are open to everyone; it's not our fault when only white people show up.* When they say *we'd like to hire more people of color, but they're just not applying.* When they say *stop making good the enemy of perfect,* and never question who gets to define "good" in the first place.

When every insufferable list of the things that make our community so great share the same two dozen bullet points: Craig Finn, skiing, hotdish, Joe Mauer, Target, the Coen Brothers, MN NICE, 3M, sculptures made of butter, the Mall of America, the fact that the Oregon trail video game was invented here and, to quote the *City Pages*, "everyone has a cabin on the lake."

To my fellow artists, remember: art is a weapon, not the war. Remember, your job is not to make people who look like you chuckle; it is to make people who look like you uncomfortable. Remember... Cece McDonald, Terrance Franklin, Fong Lee, Jamar Clark, Philando Castile, the biggest achievement gap in the country, the foreclosure crisis, teen suicides...

I don't mean to dwell on the negative. But I dwell here. No cabin on the lake. No helicopter on the stage. A cherry spoon bridge to nowhere.

3.

It's a hundred degrees outside, sirens in the distance, Big Quarters in the headphones; where are you? The neighbors are chain-linked, landing punches like mallets on meat; where are you? It's a literary reading, except the entire audience is people of color; where are you?

I do not doubt that somewhere in Minneapolis, a skinny white guy with an ironic handlebar mustache and aviator sunglasses is riding a fixed-gear bicycle to his favorite coffee shop. Or that at this very moment in St. Paul, a rich soccer mom is power-walking her golden retriever past Café Latte. But I've never met them. I've never been to a Twins game, never seen a play at the Guthrie, or gone to Rock the Garden. I'm sure they're all very nice. But the Twin Cities that I know keep me busy.

A kid gets slammed into a locker for wearing a rainbow button; where are you? A group of men pray together in the back room of a mom and pop restaurant; where are you? The students learn the footwork first, internalize the rhythm, save that spinning on your head shit for later; where are you?

Go to Tibet or Central America or India to "find yourself," if you really think that's where you're hiding. As though there weren't a million stories in every crack in the concrete here, as if the Southside weren't "exotic" enough.

The things we make invisible do not disappear; we only cloud our own perception—Minnesota nice, Minnesota passive-aggressive, Minnesota gentrifier, closet homophobe, white supremacist, bystander; open your eyes and watch Garrison Keilor possessed, irises burning blue and red, pop-locking down University Avenue, his spine a light rail, his voice an empty wind, howling like a self-fulfilling prophecy.

A Hmong teenager is shot eight times by a police officer and dies; where are you? That same police officer is awarded the medal of valor; where are you? A planted gun, an all-white jury, not guilty; where are you?

I can't listen to the Current any more. It sounds too much like history being re-written, basslines diluted, polyrhythms unified. There are days, I forget the dirt underneath the endless white of winter. There are days, I forget that race and culture are not just about blood; they are also about *blood*. There are days it is easier to believe the lie, to buy into this politely whitewashed, liberal utopia on a stick. But remember: the things we make invisible do not disappear. And the things we choose to see are not everything that's here.

A cypher blooms in the lunchroom; all of the kids love hip hop, and none of them has ever heard of Atmosphere; where are you? A group of activists march for gay rights, but it's not pride week, and they're not talking about marriage; where are you? The difference between Keith Ellison and Michele Bachmann is a single step further up Central Avenue; where are you?

Frogtown, where are you? Northside, where are you? Philips, Eastside, Little Earth, Midway, Cedar-Riverside, Uptown, Downtown, Northeast, suburbs, where are you?

Where are you?

We—all of us—are right here.

ON THE ICONOGRAPHY OF MINNESOTA AND THE TWIN CITIES

A few additional thoughts presented as an addendum to Cherry Spoon *Bridge to Nowhere.*

I'm not from the Twin Cities originally, but I've lived in Minneapolis for five years. As an outsider/insider, one thing that I've noticed is the gulf between the reality I've experienced here and the way that the Twin Cities (and Minnesota, for that matter) are presented in media.

Is there a shared Twin Cities identity? Maybe. But that identity is much more complex than what you're likely to find in one of the many "Best of the Twin Cities" lists, or "that's so Minnesotan" features, or any article, music festival, TV news segment, event, commercial, or other piece of media that seeks (whether explicitly or implicitly) to represent "the community."

For example, when the *City Pages* ran a feature on why Minnesota is the best state, it pointed to things like the Hold Steady, Brock Lesnar, Target, ski trails, hipsters, the Coen brothers, the Walker, the Mall of America, and the fact that "everyone has a cabin on the lake." When the MN State Fair has an area called "Heritage Square," it features Americana, polka, old-time and bluegrass music. Browse the *MPLS. St.Paul* magazine website and tell me whose faces you see. Whose stories are being told?

To be clear, I'm not saying that any of these symbols are bad. I like going to the State Fair. I like eating tater tot hotdish. I appreciate what The Current has accomplished. I'm just saying that by focusing so much on these symbols, we're presenting an incomplete picture. We're silencing a lot of voices. And as people who work in media, people who organize events, or just people who care about our community—we have a responsibility to do better.

Because the Twin Cities I know is a large, vibrant, diverse, complex, challenging, beautiful place. The symbols we so often encounter when talking about the Twin Cities—the sports teams, the idea of Minnesota Nice, the Cherry Spoon Bridge, "A Prairie Home Companion," etc.— these are all fine. But they're not everything. They do not represent me, or most of my friends, or many of the people in my neighborhood.

Of course, people who work in media may say *we're just giving our audience what they want*. Event organizers may say *we're just serving the people who happen to show up*.

But your audience is all white for a reason. Your board of directors is all men for a reason. Working class people don't attend meetings for your organization for a reason. Young people don't read your publication for a reason. None of this "just happens."

And this is bigger than media. When whole communities are ignored, that plays out at a policy level too. If we have an incomplete view of our city or cities, that's going to impact how we vote, how we view our neighbors, and how we build for the future.

So what can we do? In a media context, it means intentional promotion, a long-term view of audience development, creating authentic relationships in the community, and the allocation of resources needed to make all of that work. More importantly, it means hiring people—as writers, editors, board members, and beyond—who come from the communities being covered, and who reflect the diversity of our area.

I don't have all the answers, but two organizations I'd like to point to are the Main Street Project and Community Action Against Racism. Both organizations' work around media justice has been—and continues to be—inspiring. Our community's diversity is a strength, and media has a responsibility to reflect that.

THE FIRST TIME YOU SEE HIM IN UNIFORM

The first time you see him in uniform,
you bite your tongue.
He is a tall building taunting the earth to quake.

The first time you see him in uniform, you freeze,
your baggy jeans and billowing hoodie flapping
off your flagpole bones; the sand between your teeth
turns red; you smile like a claymore, triggered.

The first time you see him in uniform, you smile
like an overripe plum bursting, you smile
like velvet curtains, cut to black, polite applause, you smile
like Caesar after the shock of recognition,
after the spark of a blade between the ribs,
when nothing is left but the sadness
in Brutus' eyes. You smile.

The first time you see him in uniform, the music
is blue, midnight, suffocate, flash back.
He is helping you up after knocking you on your ass in practice.
He is waiting for you at the bus stop when you thought
everyone had left. He is smiling
like a movie star. He is allowing you to watch
him cry. He is borrowing money. He is hunting
out of season. He is talking
to the JROTC recruiter, laughing too easily like small
talk on a first date, like jingle bells on a scourge.
You are the only pallbearer,
and you are not strong enough.

The first time you see him in uniform,
you bite your tongue.
You want to spit the blood all over him.
You swallow it.

REACH

1.

On the first day of school, we make a list of the characteristics of a good poet. But this is not a poem about poetry, so all of the desks are empty, iPod earbuds dangling like dead flowers. I am alone at the chalkboard, and there is only one bullet point on that list: not talent, not hard work, not education—*ambition*.

2.

We are speedometers; usually cruising along at 20 miles per hour. A surprise birthday party bumps you up to 30. A car accident, maybe 40. Being shot at: 200. Most of us live our lives between 0 and 60. What do you think a thousand tastes like?

3.

My grandfather hates it when people use the word "awesome" to describe things that are barely above average. Like *did you see that episode of American Idol last night? It was awesome,* or *this new Drake song is awesome,* or *honeycrisp apples are the most awesome apples there are.*

God is awesome, my grandfather would say. And he is not religious.

4.

Make no mistake: this is a holy war. Beams shot from death rays into satellites and back down. Propaganda lining our cages. Six billion fingers on the button.

5.

I paid five dollars. Fifteen empty bar stools. A singer knee-deep in the stage. And if she were just a little more pretty and a little less beautiful, we'd swallow her, smiling; we'd hang her in constellation.

Confuse us with gibberish and we'll call you *visionary*. Repeat to us the slogans we already agree with and we'll call you *revolutionary*. Make some noise.

She understands that it is no difficult thing to convince 100 people to scream, that it is no victory to entertain children with sugar water and magic tricks, that it is nothing to pry a smile from the soft, dull face of America.

But she does not want our smiles. She wants to dig into the wet, grey wilderness behind them.

6.

An artist—and whether we acknowledge it or not, we are all artists—is one part clown and one part cleric. Our work is one part entertainment and one part revelation.

We are all foot soldiers in the war between giving the people what they want, and giving the people something they don't yet know they want. Between Facebook, and face. Between voting once every four years, and putting your name on the ballot. Between writing a love poem, and screaming that love poem in the Mall of America rotunda while they're walking out of Forever 21. Between running away, and running.

Because there is such a thing as awesome. It stalks in the deep, seldom-traveled back woods of culture. You might need a machete and flak jacket to get there. You might need to break a sweat. But it's there.

Don't paint my house white and tell me it's heaven. Don't bring me a sack of beans and tell me they're magic.

Bring me magic. Paint every inch of our bodies heaven. On the first day of school, do not make a list of the characteristics of a good poet. Make a list of the people who will weep when you die.

7.

We are speedometers. We are remote controls. We are dollars in tip jars in dive bars. We've seen what they have to offer. It's great. It's beautiful.

And it is not nearly enough.

CARTPUSHER
[THE FIST THAT LIVES IN YOUR NECK]

It's not rocket science. It's a ten-foot piece of rope with a hook at the end; we got three of 'em hanging in the equipment shed—one of 'em is thicker, but a little shorter; one of 'em looks thin as shoelaces but it's a good half-foot longer. If you got first pick, take that one—looks flimsy, but trust me: you'll break before it does. Try to keep up.

See, these are the days before robots, and this is a city where people leave their empty apartments, leave their empty SUVs and finally, leave their empty shopping carts. Here. For us. You can hook seven together with that rope and push 'em back in. When it's busy, grab ten. When it's hell, stack thirty up and we'll push 'em in together.

Just be careful. Because these people: they'll look right through you when they back out of those spots. When they take that corner at thirty miles per hour. When they forget that they forgot to use a blinker and cuss you out for walking through a crosswalk.

See, to that guy, we're just background noise, uncredited extras in the eighty-year long made-for-TV romantic comedy that he calls life. We are neurons flickering stupidly, infantry stomping through the dreams he won't remember upon awakening.

So make sure you wear comfortable shoes. Boots in the winter. Sneakers in the summer. Add pads as you grow older. Grow older. Learn to control a convoy of carts without that rope; just balance, coordination and will. Learn to control the fist that lives in your neck.

When these people just leave their cart sitting in the middle of a parking space, swallow. When they look right through you, swallow.

When it's fifteen below, and a straightjacket would be warmer than these flimsy company coats, and you're working a double shift because you've heard rumors of layoffs, and the dapper manager saunters up and says *how's it goin' chief?* ...swallow.

Understand: they will never understand this. The beauty of a parking lot at twilight, how the sky burns blue. The sweetness of every second when the big hand is on the eleven. The smile of the person who actually looks at you. We betray ourselves for seven dollars an hour. Our native language is white noise.

Cartpushers, cashiers, janitors, servers, bartenders: we are an army, fighting a war we don't believe in, in a country whose name we can't pronounce, but we're fighting. And we're tired. But we're fighting.

And we're losing. But we're fighting.

You get two fifteens and a half hour for lunch. Those breaks aren't for your body, though. They're for your spirit. See, with an eight-hour shift broken up into quarters, that's just four two-hour shifts.

After punching in, chatting with the MOD and putting your gloves on, you can glance at your watch and say *Wow. I'm almost halfway*

       to being halfway done

             with half

                   of half

                         of half my shift.

It makes the time fly right by.

You'll be fine, kid. Just remember: smile. You're representing the company. Remember: say hello to people when they come in.

And remember: when they look right through you, you're still there.

THE MOMMY EFFECT

The Pentagon calls it "the Mommy Effect" as if it were vertigo, as if it were faces in the white noise or déjà vu, and not something concrete like heels on hardwood or belts made of leather.

All across the country, they say, young men and women eager for opportunity but short on options, weightless, shoulders unburdened and aching for straightening, hair overgrown, overwhelming the rounded corners of youth; young men and women ready to cut themselves open for apple pie and baseball; young men and women, they say, are being snatched away by their mothers, before they can sign their names in the sand, before they can know their sweet and fitting end.

Enlistment is down, and the FBI's most wanted list is full of women in their mid-40s, high rise jeans and sequined sweaters. And they're calling it the Mommy Effect, as if umbilical cord lassos were crashing through recruiters' windows to greedily reclaim their cargo. These mothers, they say, are bleeding this country of its virility, crushing its warheads between thumb and forefinger.

And they're calling it the Mommy Effect, as if it were sweet sunsetted curses whispered in forgotten tongues through clouds of incense and swinging pocketwatches, and not something concrete like: *Kyle, if you join the army, I'll kill you myself.*

They're calling it the Mommy Effect, as if hysterical shrieking banshees wanted to dress us up in sailor suits, or suck us back into their wombs, as if these overprotective basketcases could never fully grasp just what is at stake here.

But how easily we forget: mothers have never been pacifists. They have only fought every war ever undertaken, before those wars begin and long after they have ended. They only know their children's stories too well.

Our mothers only know that sending their children away for a red and white striped greater good is not a sacrifice; it is a *sacrifice*, the ignorant, spilling the blood of the innocent, to quench the thirst of a fool's god, virgins thrown to the wolves.

And somewhere close, a virgin is sitting in a clean, air-conditioned office talking to a man composed entirely of right angles. Promises hang on the wall, ripe for plucking, and a shiny silver pen is exactly three heartbeats away from a tangled thicket of jargon, platitudes, and lovers' whispers. The man is smiling.

But exactly two heartbeats from now, a lean and muscled forearm is going to erupt from his throat, shattering that smile from the inside as a small woman, hair curlers still in and rolling pin firmly in hand, climbs out of his head like a combination of Alien and Athena.

Lightning will ricochet between her irises, and with a voice four octaves lower than God's, she will say, *You... had better get your ass... back in this house.*

The child will, of course, explode, but then assemble his scattered remains and obey.

And the sore-throated recruiter won't know how to explain it, but they're calling it the Mommy Effect.

THE PLAN

The first thing we have to do is draw up some blueprints. We'll need graph paper and a mechanical pencil, maybe one of those triangle rulers. You draw since your hand is more steady, and I'll make sure no one stands in your light. Instead of coffee we'll have hot chocolate, and around 9pm we'll break down and order Chinese food. No regrets.

Next: we gather the materials. A thousand feet of PVC pipe. Enough cheap lumber to cover our back yard. A hundred railroad spikes. A truckload of foam rubber. Two crates of candyglass prop bottles, the kind they use in movies to bust over people's heads. Duct tape, tons of it. A big jug of hydrochloric acid. Cinderblocks, at least a baker's dozen. However many dead computers and old cell phones we can get our hands on. And helium. Lots of helium. We'll make a day of it.

Construction shouldn't be too difficult. We can wear cut-off shirts and white bandanas, safety goggles perched confidently on our foreheads. We'll pack snacks. We'll dig out your old boombox, bring a stack of CDs and take turns picking them.

When the neighbors complain about the noise, we'll tell them we're building toys for orphans or habitats for abandoned puppies. If the police show up to ask about what's hiding underneath that enormous blue tarp, we'll buy them off with what's left of our nest egg.

And when the townspeople grab their torches and pitchforks, afraid that we're driving down property values with this *thing* that we're building, demanding to see it, we won't show them anything. They'll be too curious to even throw a stone.

So swing that hammer. We'll turn the music up and our hands will move like hummingbirds, every splinter melting into our fingertips, every hole bored an opening for us to spill through, every new level up a new layer in. We were born with dirty faces and steel-toed spirits so swing that hammer; climb the scaffolding with me and when we take sandwich breaks we'll look down on this inadequate city and spit.

Michelangelo said that he never sculpted anything; he simply freed the forms that already existed from the stone surrounding them. And imagining this enormous pile of materials... well, I guess we're not *really* doing the same thing as Michelangelo.

But still, sometimes, I feel ready to burst from marble, to swim through stone to meet you and explode into the world together. To build something magnificent and imperfect and greater than the sum of its parts.

But yeah, the first thing we have to do is draw up some blueprints. So draw. And when the numbers stop making sense, when the squares inside the other squares inside the other squares become so small that you feel trapped, I'll take over.

If the pencil runs out of lead you can use me: just tell me where the lines break or at what angles they bend. Tell me how delicate these curves should be and whether or not we'll be needing another spool of copper wire or shipment of bubble wrap.

It's starting to take shape—against all odds, despite the fact that we have no idea what we're doing.

It's starting to take shape.

I can see it when I close my eyes.

THE LAST WORDS OF A ROACH, UNDERFOOT

Sometimes we hear you tell your children that we're more afraid of you than you are of us.

Funny: how you never tell them about the twisting, deafening darkness mere inches from your skull when you sleep, the orgy of legs and antennae no more than ten feet from your naked toes at every hour of the day. This hell is not where we live; this hell is what we are. And we're certainly not afraid.

We may not be very smart, but our love is brilliant, twitchy and chattering inside the walls, just beyond the reach of your creeping sunrise. Our love can see in the dark.

Yes, we run when the lights are turned on, but it's not out of fear. It's just that we prefer some atmosphere—we find love in the places you don't want to admit exist and we know of a deeper bond than flowers and pop songs.

She kisses me like candy dropped under the refrigerator. She kisses me frantically with a passion too easily confused for starvation. See, over millennia we've learned that every second smiling, whispering something beautiful or feeling glorious, is a second not spent intertwined like fingers in prayer.

She kisses me like survival—through winters, through boots and rolled up newspapers, through bombs and nerve gas; our love may not inspire songs or fairy tales, but we will hold onto it long after every one of your singers and storytellers are dead and it won't be beautiful but we will still be here and no one will see us but we will still be here.

She kisses me like we won't be. Though there are days when she's halfway right, we find a way. We always have.

And we've been listening to you: you say sex can be something greater than necessity; that love can be something greater than the complex interplay of chemicals in the brain; that life can be something greater than survival.

But what could be greater than survival?

Keep your plastic-coated greeting cards, expensive shiny rocks, and whispered *I love yous* in the rain. This love has no need for props. We don't even have lips—she kisses me everywhere with everything she has.

So go ahead: turn the lights on. We dare you. What you call night is just a fumigation tent over the earth, and the stars are your last hallucination before the poison pools in your rotted lungs and overtakes you.

We will dance on your insides. Our children will inherit your homes.

And a million years from now, when your species is extinct, and every one of your songs and poems and joys and struggles and heartbreaks are forgotten, we will still be here... intertwined, fucking, a billion of us, in the dark places you'll always be afraid of.

A PRAYER FOR INDIE RAPPERS

Remember: no matter how talented you are, you will never have as many Twitter followers as Ashton Kutcher. No matter how hard you work or how many contacts you cultivate, your new music video will never have as many YouTube views as a cat riding a dog like a horse.

You are not a virtual basket of thumbs; even if you do everything right, not everyone is going to like you. And as a matter of fact, if everyone does like you, you're doing something wrong.

You are not how many CDs you've sold, how many people come to your shows or how many big-name acts you've opened for. You are not your co-signs. You are not your press clips. All of these things may matter, at some point, but they do not define you.

You are not your label. You are not your labels. You are not the extra percussion instrument, the chuckle-inducing half a mash-up over jacked beats, the one-night stand of scenester trash, the punchline, the second act on a five-act bill playing for "exposure." Even when you *are*, you're not.

In less than a hundred years, every single one of your Facebook friends will be dead. You cannot drink a drink ticket. We traffic in symbol.

So forget the blogs. Forget the local media. Forget the national media. A good write-up in *Pitchfork* is nothing compared to a good obituary.

You are not their background music, the soundtrack to their drinking/flirting/posturing. You are not a monkey, dancing for their pocket change, nor are you a god, untouchable in the artificial smoke. You are not your hype; forget your hype, whether non-existent or hyperbolic.

And of course, they're going to tell you that you are, cram it down your throat until you are drowning in their shallowness, their rules and expectations. The haters, the cheerleaders, the yes-men, the tastemakers, the gatekeepers, the unelected leaders of this sinking kingdom—they will point grenade launchers at your feet and ask you to dance. They will throw fat burlap sacks marked with dollar signs at your feet and ask you to dance.

And you may actually be good at it. But remember:

Before everything else, you are a human being standing in front of a hundred other human beings.

They are waiting for you to speak. So speak. Def Jam is never going to sign you. So speak. Rhymesayers is never going to sign you. So speak.

Say something honest. Say it because you have to. Say it like you mean it, like you're scratching your epitaph across every mile of highway between Minneapolis and Chicago, between St. Paul and South Dakota, between here and wherever this culture takes you.

Say it because no one else will, because it is so easy not to.

May the wind paint something beautiful with your ashes. May someone, somewhere, at some point in the future, find *something* to hold on to in your words. May every call have its response. May every hip have its hop.

May every hip have its...

May every hip have its...

And when you ask the crowd to scream...

LEVEL UP
[MY AUTOBIOGRAPHY AS A LEARNER]

(written as an assignment for a class)

[pre-school]
My grandmother was a teacher. And she would often grade papers while watching me. So before I was old enough for any kind of school, I *wanted* to read. I wanted to draw. I wanted to write stories. Not for any abstract love of knowledge, or to develop a skill, but just to be close to her.

This is my first memory of education—that warmth. Autumn outside the window, lots of blank paper and markers on the carpet. A smile.

This is also my first memory of privilege, which is such a dirty word to so many people, but it's not that complicated, right? It's just this. Some kind of head start. Reading the strategy guide before you play the game. Leveling up just for completing the tutorial.

[k-12]
Shop class. In a big garage adjacent to my high school. Open air, if a bit dirty. We're trying to *build* something, but more than that, we're just trying to not chop our own fingers off. There isn't a lot of room here for "visioning new possibilities." I need some metal, teacher gives me some metal. I need some wood, teacher gives me some wood. I need blueprints, teacher gives me blueprints. I assume we'll cover the drawing of blueprints in a later class.

It's just a couple of hours every week, and the weeks fly. Fingers learn to follow directions: to create from jagged, raw bits of nothing, something. To go from point A on the paper, to point B in your hands, to point C in your report card. We're building birdhouses. Wood, little metal hinges, nothing too serious, just enough to understand the relationship between hammer and nail, between heat and metal, between destruction and creation.

When I am done, I submit my work for grading. I get an F. I look down. The assignment was to build a birdhouse. I'm standing there with a broadsword in my hand, sharp as God's fingernails, smoke-grey blade, smooth wooden handle, competently crafted. I don't know what happened.

[graduation]
When you trust the process, revelations can feel like mistakes. When you buy into this system, you may thrive, you may be the one for whom the system was built, but still, your greatest victories will be framed as failures. Whatever brilliance you have access to will be dulled by the hacking and the slashing, the hacking and the slashing.

School was a game for me; to be precise, a role-playing game. I happened to roll a high intelligence, high charisma, high agility; the ability to navigate that reality with ease. My friends and I used to race each other on test day. Every A, a level up: new skills, new abilities. College was never a question; it was just the next realm to conquer.

I loved school, because school was set up for minds like mine. It doesn't mean that I'm smart. It doesn't mean that I'm not smart. It just means that I am smart in that particular context. And when a critical analysis paper happened to rhyme, or when a speech happened to be improvised, or when a birdhouse happened to be a broadsword, the things imperfections were always made. I graduated. I spoke at graduation and encouraged everyone to think outside the box. And then I went to a college that I could not afford. Level Up.

[undergrad]
There must be some kind of way out of here, said the joker to the thief; all along the ivory tower, jokers and thieves, jokers and thieves. Mostly thieves. In a role-playing game, a thief knows how to set traps. A thief has access to spaces other players don't have access to. A thief is stealthy; they always know how to cover their tracks.

For example, when you hear them say: *our department is committed to gender equity,* or *our office values diversity,* or *hey girl, I'm really into, like, intersectionality or whatever!* When they're just words, pilfered, separated from meaning, from action, from the sustained allocation of resources toward that action, it is easy to commit to them, and easier still to break those commitments. Relationships, however, are not so easily broken. The fundamental structure of the institution is not so easily broken.

I, alone, was easily broken. Between the crushing debt, the crushing class-based culture shock, the crushing reality of witnessing, day after day, the most brilliant people I know being condescended to, the best writers I know rejected for publication and grants, the hardest working people I know repeatedly stepped on by the very institution that *should* be their greatest ally; practitioners forced to drink at townie bars; social justice framed only as a neverending PowerPoint presentation and not as practice, as process; professors never saying in ten words what they can say in, you know, a million words; administrators so often not really saying anything at all; the knowledge of how to fly, without the knowledge of how to land, the campus bubble like a plastic bag over our heads... between all of this, my learning forked.

I began to "dual-class." Less a pure warrior of knowledge, and more a warrior/priest, or a ranger/mage, or a barbarian/thief. Yeah, you can't help but pick up a little thievery. At least not when you look like me.

We formed parties. In community, we learned how to swallow the knowledge that was given to us, but also to pay careful attention to its container, to its frame, to how it was prepared, to everything going on in the room and in the community around that knowledge. We remembered that they weren't the only ones with knowledge. That we had our own already. That theirs could move mountains, but that ours could move people.

They say to be educated is to be uncomfortable. Funny, how so many of the most educated people in our society are also so damn comfortable. That might be the most important thing I learned in college. Level up.

[grad school]
Don't get me wrong: there were good things too, once I learned where, how, to look. As a student activist, I learned the abstract skills of navigating personalities, collaborating effectively, framing a message; but also the concrete skills of writing a press release, designing a flyer, facilitating a meeting. I learned that no matter how precise your critique, or how much knowledge you have access to, or how unimpeachably *right* you are... it's about the work. It's about what we build. Level up.

As an apprentice educator, I learned the importance of speaking out. I also learned the importance of shutting up, the importance of listening—not just for the sake of listening, but because we all legitimately have something to contribute. The knowledge is in the room. The experience is in the room. Level up.

As an artist, I learned how to make a room move. I learned how to hustle. I learned that the impulse to create something beautiful, and the impulse to create something meaningful, and the impulse to create something popular, are not mutually exclusive. I learned that becoming a good artist is about learning... and that becoming a great artist is about unlearning. Level up.

I never really had a mentor. All of this I learned in community with dozens, hundreds of people: all leaders, all followers; all geniuses at the one thing they happened to be geniuses at.

This knowledge: not a match struck in darkness, but the act of waiting, quietly, intentionally, for my eyes to adjust.

[beyond]
I'm not a teacher, at least not in the same way that my grandmother was. I'm more likely to be named teaching artist, guest presenter, artist

in residence, force of disruption. I have no answers; I ask questions. I facilitate the creation of lists. I ask more questions. I make mistakes. I continue asking questions. I share my own knowledge too, because I do have *some*, and we're in this together. I leave room for more questions, though, for more questioning.

My favorite question is *what now?* The system is messed up— what now? Only one learning style is being engaged—what now? I have privilege—what now? I'm angry, and sad, and frustrated and overwhelmed—ok. What now?

I like this question, because I don't know what the answer is, but I know that there is one. *This* is the work. The *application* of everything we've learned and experienced, the transmutation of knowing into doing into knowing into doing—of birdhouses into broadswords.

Spoken word poems often end with that kind of callback to the primary motif, the central organizing principle of the piece. Doing this creates the illusion of completeness, kind of the macro version of a rhyme. But education is not so tidy. It continues. It expands. It leaves us unsatisfied, uncomfortable.

POLICE MAKE THE BEST POETS

Note the creative phrasing, the novel juxtaposition of words: *the officer discharged his weapon, striking the individual.* Note how the poem is so well-constructed, the newspapers print it as-is.

Note how they call it *a perfect storm of human error;* poetry is weather, after all, not climate. Note this attention to detail: height, weight, what size pants he wore, the specific model of toy gun. Poetry is, after all, about *zooming in* on these concrete particulars. Note how precise they are with their cuts: history, context, connections, trends—they focus only on what is necessary—so every time we hear the poem, it feels fresh again.

Note their mastery of repetition. Note how they show all the things they cannot tell.

A FEW NOTES AND DISCUSSION QUESTIONS

Not all of these questions will be relevant to every audience, but I wanted to include a few that might be useful to educators, aspiring writers, and anyone looking to dig a little deeper into the poems. To that end, I am not including notes or questions for *every* poem here, just a select few that might be more likely to be used in educational scenarios.

SMALL TALK
Potential Discussion Questions:
1. On one level, this is a poem about what it means to value "artist" as one element of one's identity. What identities do you hold? What elements of your personality, interests, and experiences do you hold up as important parts of who you are?

2. Are there any parts of your identity that have been misunderstood or misrepresented, or that you have felt that you had to defend?

3. The poem is also about striving to have a *deeper* conversation than we usually get to have. What are some potential obstacles to that? How might we overcome them?

Writing Prompts:
1. Describe one element of your identity that is important to you, but do it in the form of a scene—where are you, what is happening, and what is making you think about that particular element of your identity?

2. In the poem, the repetition of "ten dollars" refers to how artists give people pieces of themselves, night after night, often for just the price of a CD, book, or event ticket. Write about something in your life that is valuable in a way that transcends money.

3. Explore the idea of stereotypes and/or affirming your own identity with the prompt: "You think that I'm ____, but really I'm ____."

Additional Notes:

1. I like to start with a poem that is not explicitly "political" or social justice-oriented. A poem like this can be an entry point, a way to "seed" some points for future dialogue.

2. "Small Talk" deals with issues like identity (and how our internal identities may not always match the identities that the world places upon us, and the power of affirming one's own identity), the importance of vulnerability and sharing our stories, and even some mental health issues. While this never becomes explicit in the text, this poem is also about anxiety and introversion in the context of spaces that value confidence and conformity. All of that being said, a listener who is not ready to have those conversations can still engage with this poem as a more general piece about agency and "being yourself."

THE FAMILY BUSINESS

Potential Discussion Questions:

1. How do you think about "work?" What is the point of having a job?

2. What are the viewpoints of the two characters in this poem? Does one resonate with you more than the other? What good points do both characters make?

3. Does this poem have a central message, or is it more of a central question? How do you interpret that message or question?

4. Is there hope in this poem? If so, where is it coming from?

Writing Prompts:

1. Write about the first job you ever had—challenges, triumphs, uncertainties, etc. Can you capture what it felt like?

2. Through the metaphor of a chess game, this poem explores ideas like exploitation, expendability, invisibility, and more. Drawing from your own experience, what other images or metaphors might capture some of those ideas?

STARFISH
Potential Discussion Questions:
1. Have you ever felt tension while doing some kind of direct service work (volunteering, tutoring, etc.) and not seeing the larger institution actually change? What examples can you draw from in your own life?

2. If this poem is attempting to present a "both/and" framework (we need to do the work on a day-to-day level while never losing sight of the bigger picture), how do you see yourself plugging into that?

3. While this poem is from the perspective of an individual trying to figure out how they can make a difference, how does it change when we begin to think in more collective, community-oriented terms?

Writing Prompts:
1. Consider "the parable of the starfish," or google it if you've never heard it before. This poem is presenting a counter-narrative to that parable, but what might this counter-narrative look like in the starfish story itself? What other possibilities are there, beyond tossing them back into the sea, one by one?

TEN RESPONSES TO THE PHRASE "MAN UP"
Potential Discussion Questions:
1. The previous poem, "Handshakes," covers a lot of the same ground as this one, and its questions about gender and socialization could be used for this poem as well.

2. Are there other phrases that are not necessarily meant to be oppressive or harmful but that can inadvertently contribute to a larger culture of oppression or harm?

3. The final line of this poem points toward resistance. But if that "no" is less a final step and more a first one, what other ways can we build a culture in which people can be free to express their gender (and other identities) however they choose?

Writing Prompts:

1. Write a list poem that begins with "Ten Responses to the Phrase _____." Other examples might include "go back to where you come from" (which poet Kevin Yang tackled beautifully in his poem "Come Home") "where are you *really* from," "I don't see race," "you're being oversensitive," or any other phrase that you feel could use a response.

2. Advertisements are often crafted to play on our (often gendered) insecurities. Write a thirty-second TV commercial that satirizes this idea.

Additional Notes:

1. This is a poem that may require a content warning; see next point.

2. "Handshakes" covers a lot of the same material; choosing one poem over the other may depend on the age/experience of participants, and the facilitator's freedom around issues like cursing and "deeper" themes. As this poem alludes to suicide, rape culture, and violence against trans people, it may not be as effective an introduction as "Handshakes."

HANDSHAKES

Potential Discussion Questions:

1. What messages do we receive as children about gender? What are we taught about being a "real man" or "real woman?" How might these messages be harmful?

2. Why do these messages exist? Who might benefit from their existence?

3. How are the so-called "little things" connected to the larger realities of oppression, discrimination, and harm? Can we connect this question to the idea of "microaggressions?"

Writing Prompts:
1. Write about an experience in your life that was "small," but had a big impact on your development, and/or how you think about the world.

2. This poem isn't saying that gender isn't real or that it doesn't matter; it's saying that forcing people into very specific, narrow "gender boxes" has consequences. Think of a few of the "rules" related to those boxes, and write using the prompt "they tell me that I'm supposed to _____."

Additional Notes:
1. This is a poem that attempts to make something that is often invisible visible. Gender roles are often regarded as natural and universal, when they are in fact the products of massive amounts of information—from media, family, institutions, and society.

2. This is also a poem about insecurity and vulnerability, something that can be useful to "frontload" in a discussion or series of poems in order to diffuse authority and create space for participants to engage.

ACTION
Potential Discussion Questions:
1. This poem gives multiple examples of attitudes, actions, and cultural elements that contribute to rape culture. How would you define rape culture? Can you think of other manifestations of that culture?

2. Sexual assault and gender violence involve more than perpetrators and victim/survivors. All of us, in community with one another, can take proactive steps to disrupt violence before it happens. What might these "proactive steps" look like in real life?

3. What are some obstacles to taking those steps, and how might we work collaboratively to overcome them?

Writing Prompts:

1. Take some time to reflect on how both action and inaction are choices that we make. Whether in the context of rape culture, or racism, or any other form of oppression, we have all had opportunities to create healthy disruptions, and we have all, at one time or another, missed one of those opportunities. Write about a situation that comes to mind for you—what you did, what you could have done, or how you might handle it differently today.

Additional Notes:

1. This is a poem that may require a content warning.

2. While this is a poem specifically about sexual assault prevention, it is also a poem about critically engaging with the concept of allyship. Participants may be able to make connections to how this scene plays out in relation to other issues.

CONSENT AT 10,000 FEET

Potential Discussion Questions:

1. This poem is presenting a counter-narrative. Try to identify what that narrative is, as well as what narrative it is countering. In other words, what is the argument being made and what is the argument being rejected?

2. How do we build a culture of consent? What actions can we take (as individuals and in community with one another), and what does that look like in real life?

Writing Prompts:

1. Develop the text and/or design for a poster campaign about the issue of consent. What kinds of phrases and images might be most effective?

2. Develop the script for a YouTube PSA about consent.

Additional Notes:
  1. This is a poem that may require a content warning.

QUICKSAND
Potential Discussion Questions:
  1. What is the "thesis statement" of this poem? Does it resonate with you?

  2. Many of the actions described in this poem aren't necessarily "bad" things. Social media, for example, can be a very powerful form of communication and information-spreading, especially in a social justice context. But do you ever feel tension around doing "good" things while knowing that they are not enough? How do you process that tension?

  3. If the rope at the end of this poem is supposed to represent the idea of taking action, what might that action look like? Especially when it comes to issues like police brutality, what can we do?

Writing Prompts:
  1. Describe a scene/situation—whether from experience or imagination—that requires action. What is your thought process in this scene? How does it end?

  2. Think about what obstacles we face when action is required. If these obstacles were people, what would they be like? What would they say? How would you move past them?

Additional Notes:
  1. When performing this piece, I try to be careful to affirm that the poem is not saying that all of these actions are bad, or useless; rather, that they all exist on a continuum. The key is not finding some "answer" that will solve all of the problems related to a particular issue; it is to think critically about that continuum in a way that can lead to meaningful action.

HOW TO EXPLAIN WHITE SUPREMACY TO A WHITE SUPREMACIST

Potential Discussion Questions:

1. This poem is presenting a counter-narrative. Try to identify what that narrative is, as well as what narrative it is countering. In other words, what is the argument being made, and what is the argument being rejected?

2. When we only see racism as the acts of individual racists, and not as a set of power relations based in history, systems, and culture, what are we missing? Who benefits from our not seeing this larger picture?

Writing Prompts:

1. What might this poem look/sound like if it were about sexism, homophobia, economic inequality, etc.? Use the basic structure of the poem to address another issue; for example, "How to Explain Poverty to a Billionaire."

2. Write about something you believed when you were younger that you no longer believe. What gave you this new perspective? Can you identify a moment where this new perspective "clicked" for you?

Additional Notes:

1. Though the substance of this poem is relatively straightforward, its title can be scary for some listeners. Proper framing/introduction may be required.

THE INVISIBLE BACKPACKER OF PRIVILEGE

Potential Discussion Questions:

1. This poem is attempting to use hip hop as one lens through which we can see how whiteness impacts access to power. How does white privilege play out in other realms—education, business, social relations, etc.?

2. This is also a poem about allyship, and how being an ally is more than just believing the right things; it's about action. What are the specific actions proposed in this poem? Outside of the hip hop context, what are other "ally actions?"

Writing Prompts:
1. Describe what it feels like to have an unfair advantage or disadvantage. This can be from real-life experience, or it can be an imagined scenario like running a race with your shoelaces tied together. Use concrete imagery and details to communicate that feeling.

    a. Can you connect this scene/vignette to the ideas explored in this poem?

CHERRY SPOON BRIDGE TO NOWHERE
Potential Discussion Questions:
1. Is your community misunderstood in some way? What stereotypes are associated with your (campus, hometown, current city, etc.)?

2. Why would a community like the Twin Cities be "framed" a certain way, giving rise to stereotypes like the ones described in this poem? Where does that frame come from?

Writing Prompts:
1. Write the "real story" of a particular place that is often misunderstood.

2. A classic writing prompt is the "I am from" poem. The idea is that each line starts with that phrase, but rather than completing it with a specific neighborhood or city, you describe what that location means to you. Through sights, sounds, smells, etc., you bring it to life for a reader who may never get there.

Additional Notes:
1. This poem is about the Twin Cities; whether or not it may be useful in other communities might depend on some initial framing and context.

CARTPUSHERS (THE FIST THAT LIVES IN YOUR NECK)
Potential Discussion Questions:
1. Spoken word is about how everyone has a story, and every story has value. Even if you've never held that specific job, how could you relate to what the speaker was going through? Have you ever felt invisible? Underappreciated? Exploited?

2. How can we support each other when we have those feelings? How can community be a resource?

Writing Prompts:
1. Write about an "untold story" from your life, or from history in general, that you wish more people knew about.

2. Think about a time in your life when you were not the center of attention, but you still had something to say. You might also think about "peripheral" figures in famous scenes, photographs, etc. and explore what they're thinking.

LEVEL UP (MY AUTOBIOGRAPHY AS A LEARNER)
Potential Discussion Questions:
1. Thinking back on your own life, what have been the best parts of education, whether in or out of school?

2. What have been the worst?

3. What are the most important things that school teaches us outside of the actual substance of the lessons themselves?

4. What would the ideal schooling experience look like? What are the obstacles to that ideal? How might we overcome them?

Writing Prompts:
1. Write your own autobiography as a learner. Think back to your memories with learning, education and schools. Are there particular moments or people that stick out to you?

Additional Notes:
1. This poem sprouted from a writing prompt that I was assigned in a class taught by Sonja Kuftinec and Maria Asp. I want to give them credit and thank them for the idea.

A PRAGMATIST'S GUIDE TO FAITH
Potential Discussion Questions:
1. Even though the systems of oppression that we fight against are big, intimidating, and embedded in history, our resistance to those systems is similarly powerful. What gives you hope? Where do you draw strength from?

2. Share some everyday acts of resistance—what are things we can embed into our daily practice to contribute to the struggle for justice, equity, and peace?

Writing Prompts:
1. Trace back your own history, in the spirit of this poem, as far back as you can. You may or may not know your family history, and even if you do, that knowledge probably has its limits—so use your imagination.

2. Use the prompt "A Pragmatist's Guide to _____" to explore some other concept, idea, or issue. Especially with issues that are so often intellectualized or made abstract, how do you make them "real?"

Additional Notes:
1. The text to this poem is included in the "songs" section of this book.

SONG LYRICS

I've written a lot of songs. What follows are the lyrics for the handful of songs that ended up on my sampler project, "A Love Song, A Death Rattle, A Battle Cry." I think that these songs capture my strengths as both a line-by-line lyricist and a song-by-song songwriter as well as any in my repertoire, though as is true with the spoken word section of this book, these lyrics are meant to be supplements to the songs themselves, not standalone pieces of poetry.

All of my music is all available online for streaming and/or purchase. A full (as of 2017) discography is included on page v of this book.

A few notes on the text:

Like the poems, the songs are included here the way they were written: for songs, this means bar-by-bar. While many songs feature guest artists, I've right-aligned any text that was written *by* one of those guest artists, regardless of who raps or sings it.

Also, the songs "Lightning" and "A Programmer's Guide to Faith" both feature end-of-sentence punctuation, whereas the other songs don't. That's because these two pieces straddle the line between song and poem more than most of my work.

Notes and commentary on these songs are included at the end of this section.

DEATHBED AND BEYOND

You can call it a love song
You can call it a death rattle
You can call it a battle cry
You can call it the national anthem for your side

When I'm on my deathbed,
I'd rather have a memory of this conversation
than just a blank space in which I'd fill with fantasy
I write to turn strangers into family
I write to cultivate space, write to plant these seeds
I write to shine a little light on 'em,
see the cypher spit drip right on 'em
I write often, to see the seed change into a tree on my grave
Where others only see a stage,
I see billions of people, and billions of years
all leading up to us standing right here
And if that ain't a miracle, I am not a sinner
I'm a man tryin' to dam a river
so we're not all just water under the bridge
Give me a lake where my sisters and brothers can swim
Because I don't have a lot of close friends
I try to make up for that with a lot of far ones,
as if the light from a million little stars was
as warm as the sun on summer Sundays
I leave a CD on the counter for another someday
like... let me explain:

When I was 17, I was considered deceased for five minutes
and I remember everything, so I don't know my limits
How can you? When you see the stars like candles
unmoved by the past tense force of your last breath your
last steps never echo too far
No heaven, no hell, just an ocean of stars

And when it's all finished, you fall in it
The ripple's so small and it fits like a halo
Hey yo, I woke up in the ambulance,
the paramedics askin' *what you laughin' at?*
And after that I inhaled so hard
that a little Midwest impaled my heart
Now maybe that explains my art:
half Twin Cities, half made of stars
I've been to the other side, really
Y'all want to see what I brought back with me?

TO YOUNG LEADERS

So here's what you can expect:
a burlap sack with a dollar sign on it, or a check
They'll throw it at your feet and ask you to dance
They'll point rocket launchers at your feet and ask you to dance
I never danced, proud to play the wall and leave early
Ridin' shotgun with Circe; watch for the pigs
Watch for the cigarette vendors
Watch for the bread and circuses and remember:
Everything's for sale and everything will kill you
So don't buy it, remember who supplies it
Their teeth are syringes, eyes are blood diamonds
shinin', the patron saints of gun violence
Remember: a poem is worth more than a prayer
A prayer is a quiet conversation
A poem is an incantation, a fireball from your fingertips
It's something out of nothing, and we're listenin'
So spit it, every mic is a magic wand
And all the stage is a world
So when they ask you to dance, kick 'em in the teeth
Listen to the beat, listen to the beat...

In less than one hundred years, every single one of your Facebook friends will be dead. Your life, your impact upon this planet, upon your community, cannot be measured in likes, in plays, in CDs sold. You better recognize. You better weaponize.

So here's what you can expect:
style over substance, lust and fear over respect
I used to rap really fast,
and the kids at the shows would say "damn"
but they wouldn't understand
What you say is more important than how you say it
What you do is more important than what you say

And what you build is more important than what you do
So what you gonna build today?
Young leader, young metahuman,
young spellcaster, stay fashionin' the blueprints
Humility is beautiful, but when worse comes to worst,
remember what you're worth
Remember: people who have not accomplished
half of what you have
are going to tell you that you "work too hard"
And they'll support your yappin' but when you propose action
they'll tell you that it goes too far
But if you really want change, be prepared to make war,
whether physical spiritual cultural or something more
Because if we are the ones we've been waiting for,
what the hell are we waiting for?

The soundtrack to your life should not be background music. Wrap your poetry around a warclub. Take your most potent, battle-tested folk music, turn the bass up, and add some drums that bang. You better recognize. You better weaponize.

We are more than the sum of our parts
They are less than the sum of our fears
I think the guards are asleep at the gate,
and we got all the weapons we need right here

We are more than the sum of our parts
They are less than the sum of our fears
I think the guard is asleep at the gate,
and we got all the weapons we need right here

MATCHES

The reason that I'm not a nihilist
is someday, I want to live like in Star Trek
And I know that we'll never build starships
until we tackle poverty, war and hardship, so we fight
Overnight or over lifetimes, organize for that warp drive
and of course I realize
that we're a long way from it
But what better reason to start runnin'?
'Cause if you're gonna do the work, then it's got to be honest
because the best of us have all already been forgotten
And if you're in it for the recognition
I hate to disappoint, but if you do it right you'll never get it
Yo, we don't remember the farmer, we remember the fruit
We don't remember the inventor, we remember the boom
The impact through the eons
So I know what side of history I want to be on
I got a lot of ancestors on my side
I got an ancestor took an arrow to the chest and survived
I got an ancestor who cheated and lied
I got an ancestor who taught her children how to fight
Right? So much spirit in my corner,
can't help but color outside every border
To every ancestor who kept my song alive
I swear on your unmarked graves: I will sing it 'til I die

No friction: no flame
No struggle: no progress, no sweat
How many times do we have to win
before you realize we have not lost yet?
No friction: no flame
No struggle: no progress, no sweat
How many times do we have to win
before you realize we are not lost yet?

(deM atlaS):
What is it? What is it?
If it ain't something, then it's the other thing
that's botherin' me
Hagar the Horrible, most rhetorical lesson ever received
Was there was no need
for no money, no greed, only prophecy
shit, I'm inspired by this openness, and nothing matters;
scream at the wall, and hope it shatters
into a thousand pieces, enemy of the state
is what I became, wearin' Patti Smith's musty shoes
Rock and roll nigga I became, become
Why am I the only one who looks different?
Paint me as the new eccentric; if I had it my way
Minneapolis would be Piss Christ
suspended in air above the lakes
no one even knows the names of, and if you do,
you have too much time on your fuckin' hands
that's you pace about the room tryin' not to give a damn
Yeah, I'm kickin' down the door like I did inside the womb;
pause 'til the interlude; there's something funky to you
Forget whatever you thought you knew
'cause none of that bullshit will serve you
I'll be there in due time; until then...

No friction: no flame
No struggle: no progress, no sweat
How many times do we have to win
before you realize we have not lost yet?
No friction: no flame
No struggle: no progress, no sweat
How many times do we have to win
before you realize we are not lost yet?

There are no stories told in a vacuum
There is no prophecy lighting our way
There is just a lot of darkness to be afraid of,
so it's a good thing we are not afraid
There is no superman in that phone booth
There is no rewarding our faith
There is no one who can save us,
so it's a good thing we don't need to be saved
There are no starships in low earth orbit
No aliens to save us from ourselves
There is no voice willing to speak for us,
so it's a good thing we know how to yell
There is no chosen one, no destiny, no fate
There's no such thing as magic
There is no light at the end of this tunnel,
so it's a good thing we brought matches

THE ILLUSION OF MOVEMENT

Past the last exit, pedal to the floor, no radio,
thoughts in surround sound stereo, blastin'
with two bars in his head, ain't right, so revise, rewrite
and remember her reaction
to the first song written where she was the subject
and how her face turned red like the sunset
in his rearview, as he hits the interstate
listenin' to art that his life imitates
art imitates life imitates art
Sometimes it's hard to tell where one ends and the other starts
Especially when you're an artist
And you know words fall short,
but you're still usin' 'em regardless
He writes the verses in his head
and spits 'em to the wind, over and over again
with no beat, half a hook written to it
Now he only hopes that she'll listen to it, even though...

Halfway is as far he can get
Deep down he knows
But he's still got his hands on the wheel,
foot on the accelerator, eyes on the road

He was an amateur philosopher and part time MC
She liked to do like the dew on the leaves
and shimmer in the sunrise every Saturday
It should have come as no surprise
that she'd eventually evaporate
He didn't know what to make of her at first
and bit by bit, by accident, he started painting her in verse
She'd appear in the margins of notebooks
In between lines of poetry and logic formulas
And when they started to get close enough,

sparks flew, and for the first time they both opened up
Philosophy and poetry and music
spillin' out onto the grass at the park
where they'd laugh after dark
just to soak in the moonlight and bask in the stars
He shakes his head, and he's back in his car
Freestylin' out loud to keep from cryin'
Doin' 95, halfway to the horizon, even though...

Halfway is as far he can get
Deep down he knows
But he's still got his hands on the wheel,
foot on the accelerator, eyes on the road

She couldn't understand the paradox
when he attempted to explain it that day
That between every point A and every point B
is an infinite series of halfways
And mathematically, all movement is just an illusion
She knew it wasn't true, and she said that she could prove it
She moved in, closed her eyes, and then they kissed
The uniformity of nature crumbled in between their lips
And he knew it was impossible; it couldn't exist
but he preferred reality like this
And when she left, he didn't know what was real or true
All he knew is what he had to do
So he'll pretend that the smile on her lips exists
And seem to make some sense from this darkness
And imagine seeing her from across infinity
And dream of moving toward her regardless, even though...

Halfway is as far he can get
Deep down he knows
But he's still got his hands on the wheel,
foot on the accelerator, eyes on the road

NO CAPES

They found superman's body behind a Chinese buffet,
cape over his head, wedged between dumpsters
And I ain't dude's biggest fan, but two kryptonite bullets?
It's just messed up that he went out like such a sucker
Just got bucked like one of us would,
but it's poetic justice he'd die
in Southside Metropolis, just look up in the sky:
Ain't no birds, no planes, and no solutions,
just a permanent curtain of smog
flickered to life by light pollution
Superman was a hero to most, but he never meant shit to me
Little more than a prisoner with a life sentence
honoring us roaches with his friendship
But look who he defended: policy, property and investments
Their truth, justice and American way;
but that was never our direction,
forced into lookin' to the sky for protection that never came
as he battled robots for the status quo, not for the people
and tried to spin it into "good vs. evil"
But this is not a movie for us, tryin' to one-take life
Don't look for the sequel; look for the steeple, ring every bell
as though god had fallen and was fertilizing hell
We are not faithful;
we just know flight doesn't make you an angel

The day after superman died,
everybody stopped lookin' up in the sky
and started lookin' down at the ground
like we have been heroes here this whole time
The day after superman died,
everybody just got back on the grind
'Cause there is work to be done, yo
No capes, but we stay fly

My hero is the janitor who organizes
afterschool programs in his off time
My hero is the amateur rapper who only makes
twenty dollars but spits all night
My hero is the independent journalist
working under pressure that I can't imagine
My hero has got to be that single mother workin' two jobs
yet still findin' time to splash the canvas
My hero is the union organizer
who stays disillusioned, but he keeps movin'
He says it's for the movement,
and even if he doesn't live to see it
he'll make improvements for his kids; believe it
My hero is not a household name
She just runs a household day after day, no excuses
Her superpower's dinner made on minimum wage
for two teens and a first generation college student
My heroes are refugees
Undocumented workers sending money back home
Conscious thugs, gay rappers, and hip hop feminists
who never had shit but a dream and some backbone
And none of us wear capes; none of us will ever be president
None of us will ever be superman; we can only jump so high
But feet to the earth, we are so fly

The day after superman died,
everybody stopped lookin' up in the sky
and started lookin' down at the ground
like we have been heroes here this whole time
The day after superman died,
everybody just got back on the grind
'Cause there is work to be done, yo
No capes, but we stay fly

YOU SAY MILLIONAIRE LIKE IT'S A GOOD THING

This place is a prison and these people aren't your friends
Ain't no postal service when it's always Sunday in your head
Letters unsent, burnin' that candle at both ends
In the break room, ready to break
Halfway to broke, halfway to broken down
This job makes you nauseous; you try to hold it down
And they will take every opportunity to comment on your luck
'cause in this economy you got to be like bottom's up
even when you know it's poison, yo: you feelin' well?
Like a body that's so hungry it begins to eat itself?
Bootstraps so tight you can't admit to needin' help,
on the real, feel like hell and you want it to all stop
Jackass manager makin' small talk
Try to stay focused, you casually glance at your watch
and see that you are halfway, to being halfway
to being halfway done with half of half of your day

Punch that clock 'til it bleeds
It feels like they're tryin' to break us
They tell you to follow your dreams,
but your alarm is going off, wake up

All of my life I been lied to:
Just found out my boss makes you times what I do
and still wants to cut my hours back
to 39 and three quarters 'cause 40 gets you a health plan
And I got a feelin' I'm a need it
Losin' feelin' in my knees and my lower back
and I'm going back, trapped like a lower class clown
Hold a rat down, so we kill each other over cheddar
Keep us hungry so we never organize for nothing better
Just make it through the day, make it through the week,
make it through the month,

make a millionaire another couple bucks
What, and like that, the coffee buzz is gone
It's only 9:30, step by step with the other pawns
One square at a time, somewhere between the walking dead and
the buried alive... You can't steal what's already been stolen
You can't kill what is already dead
So if we got to be zombies, let's snatch the CEO
and see if there is a brain in his head, until then...

Punch that clock 'til it bleeds
It feels like they're tryin' to break us
They tell you to follow your dreams,
but your alarm is going off, wake up

So if you got a dollar in your pocket, put your hands in the air
Ten dollars in your pocket, put your hands in the air
If it's a hundred or a thousand that's fair
But there's no such thing as an innocent millionaire

If you got a dollar in your pocket, eat a taco
Ten dollars; buy some peanut butter and some bread
If you got a hundred or a thousand you can stock up
But a million may as well be human flesh

If you got a dollar in your pocket, drink some water
Ten dollars; you can have a beer with your lunch
If you got a hundred or a thousand, you can dig your own well
And for a million, you can drink all the blood you can suck

That dollar in your pocket is an insult
Ten dollars in your pocket ain't enough
The reason that so many of us are have-nots,
is that the haves have way too much
Let's get 'em

RIVERBED

It's hard to be the cool kid at a funeral
Skinny black tie, black shoes, it's a beautiful October afternoon
I watch a plane overhead
full of human beings who have no idea that you're...
I guess life goes on... no offense
And now I'm tryin' not to laugh, which makes me want to laugh
and I don't mean no disrespect as I step into this funeral home
like light through stained glass,
like light through black holes, like light that faded ages ago
like my phone on airplane mode
Like I don't believe in ghosts, but I swear I feel it buzz:
a voicemail from the nothing where something was
I'm still laughing; I can't pretend like I'm not sad
It's just that lack of touch is not the same as lack of contact
And that grim reaper isn't that powerful
He can't change the past and your impact is unstoppable
I don't think you die when you die
I don't think we really understand what it means to be alive
Much less existence and much less time
We think that there's no time, but maybe there's no time
And maybe memory and prophecy are intertwined
Maybe the present is a pixel in a much larger design
If the picture's resolution is a trillion by a trillion,
but the GPU display is only one by one
Well then it's easy to assume that there's nothing but the room
in which we hide, and not a whole universe outside
I don't know if any of this makes sense
I don't know if I should end it with an amen
I just know there's a river in every raindrop
and a lot of raindrops in that riverbed, I said,
I just know there's a river in every raindrop
and a lot of raindrops in that riverbed

WHOSE PLANET? OUR PLANET

(deM atlaS):
Climbin' insurmountable objects through the projects
My prospects shifted; take in what is around you kid
even the wicked, no recognition, fool
A vision of a father, single mothers holdin' it down
close to the ground; their little angels wear chain halos
Church readin' acid tablets, four quarters to a pound
You can have anything you want, even heaven
but it'll cost you something
Rain man equals the satan, you tired of waitin'
Give me what you got, what do you want?
Just a way out of this shit
In the system of division you either rich or impoverished;
martyr or the artist; brainwashed or livin' a life lost
here's a rope to hang yourself twice, cousin
Rappers are cheaper by the dozen,
frontin' they always want somethin'

Flameo hotman
Holla at the outdated slang and the cadence we rock with
Rhyme bender, soul bender, beat bender, watch it
Conscious is never enough, who rock better than us?
Who not ready to run, but got both feet planted
like whose planet? Our planet
Bigger than the streets that we spill through kid
Bigger than the lies that they try to kill you with
It's something like a phenomenon
My rhymebook like the necronomicon
While they blah blah blahin' on and on
We got spirits ready to call upon, c'mon
Try and stop me
I'm somewhere between Brother Ali and Ed Bok Lee
Like a indie-rap Wolverine: I'm the best at what I do
but what I do is nice
So tell your favorite rapper think twice

Picture me smilin' on the cover of the Vita.MN
with two chains, boots, boomerang on my item list
I made it this far with only one heart
This is hardcore mode: we only got one life to live
So I'm a write to this light within, pencil in my iron fist
Flyin' while they American Idolin'
You can't decipher the cypher, that's what a cypher is:
Always breaking, never broken; take it higher
It doesn't take much and that's messed up
They use the culture to stress and oppress us
But while everyone was tryin' to censor the fire
I skipped flame, spittin' out a mouthful of spiders
And you don't think this is magic?
With one verse I can turn a curse to a classic
A spell to a song, or an incantation
to a taste of forever from your favorite station
Like, your potential is limitless
The mana bar's full, so why you still swinging that little stick?
Knowin' damn well you could unleash hell
if you found what you believed in and whispered it
into existence like a wizard spittin' lightnin' off of his lips
Don't bite the bullet now and call it a kiss
'Cause if your callin' is this, better ball up your fists
Thick skin, carry a blade at all times
'Cause every day is a mosaic of fault lines
And when the pain hits just taste that rawhide like RAH

THE FOURTH WALL

The day breaks through my third floor window, hard
A cell phone alarm in every shard
of sunlight, creepin' through the cracks in my consciousness
A dream slips away, and I'm awake, like "damn"
Ain't no snooze button for these birds
or the sense that sleep is something to be earned
Don't forget that; a billion other people tryin' to rise too
Tumble out of bed, the Pharcyde's in my iTunes
Orange juice for breakfast
Grab my rhymebook, full of meeting notes and checklists
Maybe today I'll have time to write a new song
if I freestyle my life, it's like that
Sixteen bars into a bottle I can't move on
Waitin' for the waves to write back
and I can't remember my dreams now, it's be crazy to follow
They say "seize the day" ...maybe tomorrow

Wake up in the morning sayin' "break a leg"
because you know all the world is a stage
But if you could tear down the fourth wall
and talk to the audience, tell me what would you say?

Gotta pay these bills, still wonderin' what my best option is
Drownin' in a stream of class consciousness
So much respect to the janitors, props to the drivers
Peace to the teachers and survivors
of nine-to-five shellshock, combat fatigue
Overworked, underpaid, underclass battling
the evil not so much scary as monotonous
Every day an anticlimax, underwhelming apocalypse
We keep on spinnin' and spinnin' fully intendin'
to grip on to every minute and live it up to its limits
From beginnin' to endin' we get to livin' and sinnin'

and slippin' back into the grip of these material wishes
It got me wishin' I could stop, and grab a hold
I ain't trying to wake up tomorrow and be old
And I ain't lazy, I like workin'
But they say "seize the day," and I'm a night person

Wake up in the morning sayin' "break a leg"
because you know all the world is a stage
But if you could tear down the fourth wall
and talk to the audience, tell me what would you say?

Sittin' in the frame of the big picture
lookin' out at every step I took in the story
I'll seize the day with both hands finally,
knuckles bleedin' freedom: good morning

                                                    (Lydia Liza):
                                    Feet are calloused from the run
                                    Looking back on what I was
                                    I can feel how far I've come
                                    I can feel that I'm not done

And still I can't find the place where I woke up
Too busy feedin' the cycle of seasons
breathin' the poison that slowly chokes us
Cog in a machine and I'm fallin' into a dream
And we're drownin' in our unconscious but I ain't callin' it sleep
My insomnia is hard-fought
'cause I know the sooner I fall asleep,
sooner I'll hear alarm clocks
Make 'em all stop, whisper melodies of "no chance"
Watch the gladiators melt into a slow dance
And pain is tellin' me to hold back
but I've seen too many faces in the night
spillin' from the smokestacks
The time-clock is a time-bomb tickin'

we're livin' until we're flipped inside a prison or a pine box
Why not? Smiling reflections in razor blades
but they won't let me die; I ain't got enough vacation days
says the manager, guilty, to the gallows with 'em all
and I'm the janitor strugglin' scrubbin' shadows off the walls

THE HERO

Look up in the sky: it's a bird, it's a plane
It's a person to save all we've made
It's just your average everyday super-powered superhero
flyin' through the sky and all tryin' to save people
Faster than a bullet, tougher than a tank,
runnin' like a train, nothin' in his way; he's come to save the day
from the evildoers and the villains fillin' up the street,
the shepherd to stop the fox from killin' all the sheep
A million on his beat, he watches the whole city as it sleeps
A guardian to keep the peace on the streets
The newspaper reads "a hero arises"
A new hope for a people in crisis
Evil is hidin' and crime is down
something like twenty five percent; that ain't no minor step
He won't face the spotlight though, he keeps it humble,
silently watching over his concrete jungle...a hero

Everybody have no fear
Who we're waiting for is finally here
to do what he needs to do
and make the city safe enough for me and you
Look up in the sky: it's a bird, it's a plane
It's the one who's going to save us

It was a dark night; it was the perfect crime
Makin' the getaway, he thought he heard a guy
behind him, and suddenly he's on the ground lyin'
his hands tied, and a man's standin' beside him...

Well aren't you the hero, arrive to the emergency
C'mon man, I stole a hundred dollars from a burger king
But the city's "safer" I suppose
Well as long as I got caught, I want you to know:

Listen: I ain't the bad guy; I'm just hungry
and minimum wage is not enough in this country
If you want to fight crime, but you don't go for the roots,
well you can win every battle, but all in all you'll lose
You see crime comes from poverty, lack of opportunity
and poverty is policy in too many communities
And yeah, you're proud of all the thieves you've stopped
but dog, all the real thieves already made it to the top
And what you need to know, the real evil yo:
Politicians and CEOS
And you can catch every petty criminal like me
But can you put food on the table of a starving family?
Can you get my job back at the factory?
Or healthcare for my mama's sickness that she's battling?
War, poverty, environmental catastrophe:
those are the crimes, why the hell you after me?

Everybody have no fear
Who we're waiting for is finally here
to do what he needs to do
and make the city safe enough for me and you
Look up in the sky: it's a bird, it's a plane
It's the one who's going to save us

A month passed and the hero disappeared
and the people startin' askin' *what's happenin' here?*
Ski masks are down, they proceed with caution
And now crime is up, and the streets is talkin'
Did he leave his office? Is he gone for good?
Did he finally decide he did all he could?
Until one day, middle of autumn
leaves fallin' the hero came back for a press conference...

Ladies and gentlemen, people of the city
I'm sorry for my absence, really, I apologize
But all this time, I had to do some thinkin'

about the crimes that I did and didn't authorize
Just call this a change of heart,
or better yet a change of perspective
See I'm a change directions
And I know fightin' crime is hectic
but I see now: the police don't fight the real evil, they protect it
And I'm sick of pretendin'
that only poor people have bad intentions
Yes I fight crime, and I intend to beat it
'cause I will fight the conditions that created it and feed it
And there's some evil here I can feel it
and I'm not going to rest 'til it's defeated, believe it
So if you'll excuse me I got to fly out
See, I got some business at the White House

BREAK

The new kid has a belly full of fireworks
and this school has no shortage of sparks
That new kid was me, five times in five years,
with a smile like kindling, skin like dry bark
and flint in my heart; every day was inferno;
90 college-ruled black pages in my journal
Redacted, redacted, redacted
No surprise that I learned how to write with matches No surprise
that I learned how to burn in silence
No surprise what I learned I ain't learn in classes Just learned a few
words like magic
Learned there's a rebirth in every urn of ashes
Let those fireworks be your paintbrush
Thin line between arsonist and artist
That fire inside can burn everything down,
but it can also light your way through the darkness

(**Kristoff Krane**):
Migrate, instinct, surface, searching
deeper, we dig, seed emerging
teacher, student, secrets, perfect
eager, nervous, dream big

It's just another closed door on the old invisible me
Character flawed by the ghost that lives in my genes
So sore in the bones, so soar in the sky
Stone cold to the touch, so bored I could cry
me, me me me me me a river
through a mountainside, my oh my make me remember
what it's like to shiver in the pits of December,
the center of the circle of influence I surrender
to, to the flame that I bow to:

it told me to be silent, so I screamed; it was sound-proof
Raindrop, butterfly, chaos, chameleon
Environment shaped, different colors disobedient
Yeah, and I'm tryin' to act my age,
back pressed tight against the wall of a cave
Birthdate states 1983, that means I'm twenty-eight
point-six-five-four-two-thirty-nine billion years away
from my birth place; stayin' on this earth takes time
willpower by the urge of survival,
king of the hill, kill or be killed;
they tell me like that's the only way to fly out of bird cage
I'll sing my heart out 'til I'm in shock
Put the key in the lock; I'd rather clip my wings
than fly in a lost flock, who fights dirty,
in flight searching, for a surface that's perfect

Wash me 'til I'm clean of what I've done
Hold me like you need someone to love
Kick me like a habit I'm a drug
Fix me 'til I break what you made up
Wash me 'til I'm clean of what I've done
Hold me like you need someone to love
Kick me like a habit I'm a slave
Fix me 'til I break what you made up

An open letter to myself at fifteen, fallin'
Don't wait to grow wings or nothin' just hit the ground runnin'
The pit of your stomach is a star collapsing
Your fist is a lit wick, far from lasting
so act, a little known fact:
everything is flammable if you got the right kind of match
So if you find a rough patch in your life it's
just another place you can strike it
We're all capable of so much
We're all waiting for a sign that's never going to show up
We're all made from the same dust

We're all convinced that it's paydirt, can you blame us?
We're all lasers pointed at the sky
Like any one of us can hit it, but can you make it ignite?
We might be prepared to lose,
but we are also prepared to fight, let's go

Wash me 'til I'm clean of what I've done
Hold me like you need someone to love
Kick me like a habit I'm a drug
Fix me 'til I break what you made up
Wash me 'til I'm clean of what I've done
Hold me like you need someone to love
Kick me like a habit I'm a slave
Fix me 'til I break what you made up

An open letter to my enemy: you are stronger than I'll ever be
and I don't measure up in any way that you can measure me
So take my lunch money, and take the love from me
and replace it with hate 'til I break, but I'm done running
Whatever the better measure of strength,
a bully ain't nothin' but a nosebleed
Though if it were as simple as keeping your head up,
a lot of brothers and sisters wouldn't never have left us
How do you miss this?
Nine suicides in two years in one school district
They say kids will be kids
I say bigots will be bigots; their kids will be just as ignorant
But we are a community
and stand together when it's not right, and not fair
If you want to change the world, change yourself
just don't think for a minute you can stop there

LIGHTNING

I was struck by lightning.
Not as a figure of speech; I was literally struck by lightning.
It smells like a hospital on fire,
like the cleanest smoke you can imagine,
like spring water pulled apart by the atoms.
It smells like recycled air on an airplane crashing.
What are the odds? It didn't give me superpowers,
so I guess I got to take my chances

with small talk, weather reports and high traffic,
with time clocks, and time bombs, and time passing.
When I'm not here any more will my planet
even notice my absence?
I swear, some days are like carvin' your name into the capitol
with just your fingernails while the politicians laugh at you,
and some days are worse.
I want to leave a legacy so you'll remember me for more than this
verse, please:

hold your applause.
Hold it forever.
There is so much that keeps us apart,
and so little that holds us together.
But whatever that is we're going to need it.
It's going to get worse before it gets better.
And it only gets better when we do better.
And we only do better when we fuse together, yes:

there is no progress without struggle,
whether you're an activist or just a kid in some trouble.
A student graduating with debt, a single mother distressed,
A little brother repressed, dripping the sun as it sets

into a habit hidden under the bed,
while four walls echo something I said;
when dark clouds gather, remember to just fight back;
not everyone can be touched or struck like that

and survive.
But you did.
You still got a spark inside,
so use it.
See, I've learned a little bit about energy.
I've learned when it enters you, it loses charge.
So the negative and positive are worth the same amount:
the passion and the pain, the smiles and the scars.

Whether you lost your job or won the lottery,
that energy enters you like a lightning bolt,
and no matter how dark its origin,
once it's inside you, it's yours to control.
So what this means, is that those
who've been through the most have the most to let go.
There is strength in our anger, power in our pain,
even beauty in the hourglass' grains.

It all depends on how we use it.
Some people make music. Some people make excuses.
Some people make enemies. Some make-believe.
Some people make the most of every tragedy.
And me, well I just want to make a scene.
Ain't going to patiently wait for my pain to bury me.
Ain't going to waste all this energy chasing popularity
or prosperity; I'd rather stand tall in solidarity

with everyone we've lost, because they're never lost,
and every one of y'all who stay forever strong,
and we'll build basslines out of thunder,
rap to the rhythm of the rain, and dance on the little bit of space

that we have and build something lasting
as this empire's collapsing.
And when they ask me to come along quietly,
I'll say how can I quit? I got lightning inside of me.

(Chastity Brown):
I was there, I confess
Wind was shakin'
time was movin'
ever slowly; I was there
on the floor, saw the door,
grabbed the page, wrote some more,
found the rage, wrote a score;
I was there when lightning broke
I was there when lightning broke

DRAGONS

It doesn't have to be perfect to be alright
and I ain't sayin' to settle,
I'm sayin' love is all learnin' to see it right, right?
And lord knows the situation is tainted
but I can't imagine amateurs takin' your place it
ain't no fairy tale, and baby I ain't slayin' no dragons
'cause maybe, I'm in love with one
And together we can terrify the villagers
and burn their homes down;
profound how we run amok
And yo something's up here, it's a spark clear in the darkness
Regardless of fightin' we're still far from dividin'
One heart in defiance to science and common sense
We don't belong together, I see it, but I ain't gone yet
And neither are you, it's that attraction
Dancin' to the aftermath, music loud, laughin'
I'm glad that you're fine with me
It ain't the song that played on our first date but it's kinda pretty

A match made in heaven doesn't burn right
Destiny doesn't pay the rent
And I don't remember all the words to the song,
but I believe in them a hundred percent
A match made in heaven doesn't burn right
Destiny doesn't pay the rent
And I don't remember all the words to the song...

We will meet in the middle of the riot
We will meet in the free falling plane
We will meet in a dark little corner of hell
We will meet one another halfway
We will meet in the warzone
We will have the time of our lives
We will push our hospital beds together
We will meet as the meteor ignites the sky

So one two, one two
It's like one for every dream that ain't gon' never come true
and two for me and you, it's love but it's luck too
Sayin' it through misery and gritted teeth: I love you
Everything we've come through, memories are heaven sent
All the bad made the good all the more resonant
And I ain't hesitant to say it
This relationship's a monster I'm confident we created
And these last days, remind me that your spirit never faded
When facin' a breakin' point: made a choice
Right brain tellin' you that we should make love
Left brain tellin' you that we should break up
and just stay in bed choosin' not to wake up
wrapped in the daybreak, no one to save us
floatin' away but never reserved
I'll keep singing our song, even if I can't remember the words

A match made in heaven doesn't burn right
Destiny doesn't pay the rent
And I don't remember all the words to the song,
but I believe in them a hundred percent
A match made in heaven doesn't burn right
Destiny doesn't pay the rent
And I don't remember all the words to the song...

We will meet in the middle of the riot
We will meet in the tree falling plane
We will meet in a dark little corner of hell
We will meet one another halfway
We will meet in the warzone
We will have the time of our lives
We will push our hospital beds together...

A PRAGMATIST'S GUIDE TO REVOLUTION

I'm fightin' on until my life is gone,
even when my version of health insurance
is orange juice and tiger balm,
even when my attention is so divided
between rappin' and writin' and activism and survivin'
And at any given time, so many of us are new to this,
but you ain't got to stop listenin' to Ludacris
And you ain't got to dress a certain way,
ride your bike in wintertime,
shop at the co-op or ever turn away
from who you really are; this movement doesn't need perfect
it just needs us to start workin'
Radical means you have hope,
and sometimes you vote for it, most of the time, though, you don't
So this is for the ballot, the bullet, the bulletin and the boycott,
for the hand-to-hand, and the door to door
More and more, it's growin' in popularity;
we don't say *peace*; we say *solidarity*

With this many hands we could start a fire
With this many hands we could start a war
With this many hands we could build something beautiful
With this many hands we could do much more

I got a friend who ran for city council and he got elected
I got a friend who ran for school board and got rejected,
but in the process, learned about the process,
wrote a couple grants, now she runs a non-profit
I got a friend who never went to college,
but knows the first and last names
of everyone in his housing project
It starts with the basics;
I got another friend who throws parties in his basement
And basically, that's just the baseline:
Power is a hundred people in the same place at the same time

Right? But what are you going to do with it?
I got a friend who knows what the revolution is,
and knows that though the music is beautiful,
it's the people that it brings together who are better,
and the senators and representatives will only bend
to the will of the real changemakers: my friends

With this many hands we could start a fire
With this many hands we could start a war
With this many hands we could build something beautiful
With this many hands we could do much more

Shout to Howard Zinn
Have you ever seen the world through a bomb sight?
Have you ever prayed through a darkness beyond night?
This song might be a bunker-buster, daisy-cutter,
thermobaric American, crazy proletarian
But when you boil in the belly of the beast it's scary,
so hack out by any means necessary
They're going to call it *terrorism* either way,
so you can run for the clear, or give 'em something to fear
C'mon, and I ain't talkin' 'bout bombs
I ain't talkin' 'bout Bibles, Torahs or Qurans
I'm talkin' 'bout the god that lives in your feet
when you're walking,
the god that lives on your lips while you're talking,
the god that lives in your fist when you fight for
something worth fighting for
This whole life is war, and the first step to victory:
like Toki Wright said: *know the history*
An injury to one is an injury to all, understand me
They step up to your cousin, you run and go get your family
So when they step to you on some realness,
you got the whole city risin' up, climbin' up that double helix
Your job is to protect your family; and your family is everyone Power
to the people: give it a chance
'cause it'll work; it's the only thing that ever has

SPIRIT BOMB

I never did the graffiti thing; she just did it in spurts
like every few months she'd get to feelin' the urge
and then she'd disappear, leavin' her purse at my place
with a backpack full of pilots and spraypaint
And I never went with her, I just figured that
little act of throwin' a tag up was similar to therapy,
a spiritual journey for just a little bit of clarity
in a world full a heartbreak and insincerity
Apparently I was right; she'd tell me stories
of how peaceful the city was at that time of night,
how shadows crept up from the deep city streets
and splashed up on the walls
while the people would sleep
And she'd frequently speak of the need to release energy,
and I loved to hear everything, see
I had walls all around me, and I can't say enough
to thank her: she couldn't knock 'em down,
but she tagged 'em up

One for the root, two for the tree,
three to infinity for all of the leaves
We let go and float on a fall breeze,
and drop when we hear that beat
See it goes like one for the root, two for the tree,
three to infinity for all of the leaves
We let go and float on a fall breeze,
and drop when we hear that beat

And we didn't stay together but we left on good terms;
stood firm, both knew it just wasn't gonna work
I've just always had a thing for artists;
regardless of other circumstances, the art was romantic
My heart was attracted to lost souls, how come?

Well with us, ain't no such thing as a found one
We drifted, to connect to something deeper
whether painted on a wall or bumped through speakers
like, another day, another tag, another rap,
another chance to touch someone in ways
that even lovers can't
And that's as real as it gets; now my sleepin' is stressed
when writer's block got me feelin' depressed
but we press on, 'cause someone's got to write these songs,
and a bare wall without life is wrong
So every time I see her four letters I remember:
that graffiti fades, and songs can't play forever
but they don't have to, they never really did
See this is not another sad song
and for whatever it's worth, I'll still see her tag
long after all my walls are gone

And it goes like one for the root, two for the tree,
three to infinity for all of the leaves
We let go and float on a fall breeze,
and drop when we hear that beat
It goes one for the root, two for the tree,
three to infinity for all of the leaves
We put our names on the walls,
and our hearts on our sleeves
and we drop, we drop

ONE OF THESE MORNINGS

I walk to work in the mornings
yeah that's right, a nine-to-five to supplement
the little earned from performin'
Verse to the chorus, meat to the dessert; this work
is worth ten minutes walkin' all immersed in words
I'd meditate, but see I kind of love that chaos
I got wings, but I ain't in no rush to take off
And you ain't got to wonder what my angle is:
not quite a hero, but more than a protagonist
Tryin' to relearn my language by listenin'
and talkin' out what my mission is
Let me talk to April, on her way to class,
thinkin' 'bout a way to pass
when tuition is risin' high and she's fadin' fast
Let me talk to Kevin at the corner store
about everything we'd do if we'd only had a quarter more
Let me talk to my grandfather,
even though I know what he's going to say
I'd like to hear it anyway
'cause one of these mornings
you're going to rise up singing

Let me talk to myself, and let 'em stare I don't care
Let me talk to the walking biography that's Javier
Nineteen, self-educated, laughin' at college
Readin' *Wretched of the Earth*, writin' raps in the margins
Let me talk to that aspirin' artist
and warm my hands on the fire that's started
Let me talk to Rianna: pretty voice, wants to sing,
but her parents keep saying:
graduation, then marriage, then baby carriage
then what? Let me talk to the person who ends up
at some dive bar listenin' tippin' her ten bucks

And though we ain't that close,
let me talk to God—just allow a couple minutes to pass
We don't always get along 'cause I'm livin' so fast
but he likes me 'cause I ain't always kissin' his ass
And let me talk to Tommy
We don't talk much, so I'll just say sorry, and I'll tell him that
one of these mornings
you're going to rise up singing
And one of these mornings, I swear I'm gonna figure out
how to catch your eye with my light before it flickers out
'Cause I can live without the fortune and the riches
as long as when I die I leave a corpse that made a difference
Let my pallbearers be six ex-girlfriends
who kept in touch and stayed on good terms 'til the end
And everyone I've ever talked to will either be in attendance
or waitin' for me at the entrance
Because I wish I had the courage to say more
to every single stranger that I've met at every airport
but I'm scared or just shy of where our stories intersect it's
me in these three minutes and forty-one seconds
Freedom in connection, blessed to even taste it
'Cause life ain't short, it's just a lot of people waste it
and I'll be damned if I'm going to keep my mouth shut
Rise up and sing a song right or wrong 'cause
one of these mornings
you're going to rise up singing

THIS IS THE OPPOSITE OF A SUICIDE NOTE

I met the devil in the Midwest,
dressed like a promoter, floatin' on the limelight,
eyes like supernovas,
his shoulders: the Minneapolis skyline
Needless to say, I turned the opposite way,
not welcoming tomorrow today;
I mean I gotta relay a legacy before they off me
I am not tryin' to leave yet, I am not sorry
So I'll assemble an army of rappers
and spoken word poets and activists and dancers
and yeah, they'll be half an hour late,
but they'll show up eventually
and each will have a chapter
And after the manuscript we've built is assembled,
I'll scribble on the last page *dedicated to the devil*
Book's heavy as religion embedded in blacktop;
first page, eighty two point font in caps lock, screamin'
This is the opposite of a suicide note;
pin it to your chest, sing it under your breath,
tattoo it to your children, graffiti the fortress,
scrawl it on the tip of every nuclear warhead
Said this is the opposite of a suicide note;
let it raise the fallen, call to arms, instill fear
Let my life be as jagged as my penmanship
'cause shit, if you're hearin' this now, it means we're still here
And my advice is to love your life,
and if you don't have a reason, keep breathin' out of spite
'Cause that's a form of self-love too;
some days I fight just so I can tell my demons *hey, fuck you*
This is the opposite of a suicide note;
my roots too deep in this earth to move
I made allies of axes, friends out of chainsaws,
so how the hell you gon' tell me to take off?

I will stay on the table 'til after the eight ball
sinks for the last hustler's pay off,
drinks on the house then
and then we'll slide out with the bubbles
in the champaign fountain
'Cause this is the opposite of a suicide note
If I've ever said anything right, make it this
make a fist for something bigger than a paystub;
dedicate this to everyone who never gave up
even in the face of oblivion, we crack a half smile and
daps to the fallen, songs through the silence
And in the rain, never put the hoodie up; we stay fresh want to feel
every drop to the depths
So yes, let's assemble an army of teachers
and homeless children and union organizers,
cops and drug dealers, prostitutes and preachers
and factory workers and students and truck drivers
and doctors and soldiers and mothers and ghosts
and everyone can add their own chapter
And after the devil comes for me, with a smile and a receipt,
and pockets like black holes as wide as they are deep,
I'll hook my arms inside yours and tell him sorry
This is my poetry; this is my army
We stand together, and live every word we wrote
All I got to say, is *not today*
This is the opposite of a suicide note

REVOLVER

She is standing just outside a doorway
She is watching the old road to the sea
She is closing her eyes
She is saying goodbye in a language that she doesn't speak
She is reaching, it is dawn, it is dusk, it is pitch black
It is raining still from a cloudless sky
The stars burn bright in the afternoon blue
The moon's waxing and waning, it's full, it is new
it is falling... She is calling out a name
A chorus in her throat, a thousand sounds overlapping
Every name she has lost along the way
Every face she will lose in the future she is standing
alone, with a child, with an in-law, with a village
in a desert, in a suburb, in the snow
Alone once again, they are coming to take her boy away,
so away he'll go

(**Claire de Lune**):
I just want to love you right
I just want to love you right
I just want to love you right
Why's that such a crime?

She is standing just inside a doorway
She can still taste the salt in his name
She is African, Asian, American, European
although her hands are always the same
She is praying to gods and angels that flicker
in and out of existence, to spirits that laugh
How many wars has it been? How many prayers
like paper boats drifting to never come back?
They have taken him to fight
in forests in deserts in oceans in jungles in towns
With a spear, with a bow, with a sword, with a rifle

with a computer, it's the future that's mowing him down
The past is chewing on his leg; the present is licking its lips
She is thinking of him all alone
Once again, they are coming to take her boy away,
so away he'll go

It ain't going to work out,
yeah I've known it from the start
Just 'cause you know it with your mind,
don't mean you know it with your heart

And I just want to love you right
I just want to love you right
I just want to love you right
Why's that such a crime?

She is standing away from the door now
He is sleeping in a back room, heavy
They are creeping up the road like daylight
just as they have a million times already
But she remembers her trembling hands now
She remembers his million faces
So many sons, extinguished for what?
They are serving for words they have never tasted
She is holding her heart in her hands now
Each chamber is **full, it is cold**
She remembers this story but knows
that it changes a little every time it is told
She remembers the knock on the door
The morning is dead, its ashes are scattered
Once again, they are coming to take her boy away,
so she cocks the hammer

I just want to love you right
I just want to love you right
I just want to love you right
Why's that such a crime?

A PRAGMATIST'S GUIDE TO FAITH

This is the art of drawing breath,
of making visible what has been invisible.
This is a pragmatist's guide to faith.
This is singing when you don't know how to pray.

Welcome to this space; know that you are not welcome here.
We are all trespassers; we are not welcome here.
This universe would like nothing more than for you to not exist,
and the proof is in the history you live; tell me this:
what are the odds that this planet would appear
in just the right place, with the right atmosphere and geology?
What are the odds that life would suddenly spark
in the darkness, from the carcass of this planet to a colony?

What are the odds that this anomaly would spread?
What are the odds it would survive and stay ahead
of volcanic eruptions, meteorites and earthquakes;
that first drum, first beat, first rhythm, first break,
first time the notes broke to form a system?
You could hear the first melody, the first multi-celled organism.
What are the odds this first environment to harbor life
would meet another; maybe fight or maybe harmonize?

But either way it would evolve.
So what are the odds it would evolve to walk and not crawl?
To fly but not fall? To survive every single mass extinction?
What are the odds of your existence?
How many generations did it take to make you?
How many plagues, wars and massacres conspired
to uproot your family tree and salt the earth around it?
How many ancestors carried your fire?

How many farmers made it through the famine?
How many runaway slaves got away?
How many soldiers conscripted deserted?
How many times did that chain almost break?
How did your great-great-grandparents meet?
What was the song playing when you were conceived?
Is it inconceivable: the happenstance inherent in
this life you have inherited?

Some see the elegant complexity of bodies,
or the natural beauty of the planet and they say it's godly.
There's got to be divine intelligence behind it all
because the odds that you would make it on your own are so small.
But me? I see millennia trying to murder you.
I see a thousand generations of pain and fear.
I see struggle inscribed into your skeleton.
And I see you still here.

Ancestor armor. Star-crossed survivor.
An unwelcome guest in a hostile environment.
Defiance is your birthright, fire from the first time
you drew breath, a smile on your face.
Welcome to this space; know that you are not welcome here.
We are all trespassers; we are not welcome here.
So if our drawing breath is blasphemy, sin or treason,
let's keep drawing breath until there's nothing left to breathe in
We are the codes that our ancestors still speak in.

NOTES AND COMMENTARY ON THE SONGS

DEATHBED AND BEYOND

This track is a medley of three different songs. I've always been a big fan of remixing, re-situating, and sometimes straight-up reusing songs and verses. Some people raise an eyebrow at that, but it's just part of my process. I'm not the type of MC who goes on tour and hits the same cities once every year for ten years; I'm constantly in new places, meeting new people, and if I'm going to sell anything to them, I want it to be the best representation of what I do. That's what this sampler mix is all about, and this song in particular represents that philosophy.

Also, we only got to work with Haley Bonar for an hour or two, but she's one of my favorite singer/songwriters in the world. I wrote this hook, and she ran with it in a way that was absolutely perfect—both for the song it originally appeared on, and for the intro to this mix.

Produced by Big Cats
Additional vocals by Haley Bonar
"The National Anthem" appeared on "An Unwelcome Guest"
"The Ripple" appeared on "Don't Be Nice"

TO YOUNG LEADERS

Big Cats is one of the most talented producers in indie hip hop, and this might be the strongest, most singular song in our history together. For me, this was an ideal canvas for just letting out a lot of pent-up anger and frustration. But beyond the cathartic elements, I'm proud of how this song came together on a poetic level too. It's big and loud, but it's also weirdly beautiful, which is probably a great way to describe our music in general. I still perform it pretty much every time I play a live show, even when some of the "bigger" elements in the song scare people.

Like much of my writing about art (including "REACH" and "A Prayer for Indie Rappers," among other poems and songs), this song uses an artist lens to explore something that applies to everyone; the lessons here are explicit if you happen to be an artist, but my hope is that they transcend that.

Produced by Big Cats
Appeared on "You Better Weaponize"

MATCHES

Sifu Hotman is a collaboration between me, MC deM atlaS, and producer Rube, and this is my favorite song of ours. It features two of the best single verses I've ever written, plus a scene-stealing deM atlaS verse, plus a gorgeous bassline loop. This song also ended up being featured as "the weather" on an episode of *Welcome to Night Vale,* which introduced our music to thousands of new people.

This song, along with "To Young Leaders," is pretty much my personal philosophy crystallized into a couple minutes of music. It's the kind of thing that probably wouldn't sound right in a spoken word poem, but just works (at least for me) as a song.

One other note: it took me a long time to figure out that verses that feature some kind of repetitive conceit are super powerful. I'm always kind of surprised that more MCs don't take advantage of that.

Produced by Rube
Additional words/vocals by deM atlaS
Appeared on "Sifu Hotman: Embrace the Sun"

THE ILLUSION OF MOVEMENT

"A Loud Heart" happened almost on a whim; me and Claire just both knew Big Cats, met in the studio, and decided to throw a few acoustic rap songs together. It ended up being one of the most popular musical projects I've been a part of, something people still stop and ask me about fairly frequently.

This is actually a re-interpretation of an older song of mine; I think I read about Zeno's paradox when I was a teenager and wrote a terrible poem about it; that poem then later morphed into a pretty good song not only about love, but also about fighting losing battles in general. So the lesson is to never throw away your first drafts.

Guitar and additional vocals by Claire de Lune
Appeared on "A Loud Heart"

NO CAPES
If I have a signature song, it's probably "No Capes." It captures the whole "love song, death rattle, battle cry" balance as well as anything I've written—it's weird, it's political, and I like to think that it's also relatively down-to-earth and human.

People always ask me whether I prefer rapping or spoken word. Usually, I lean toward spoken word because I like having audiences 100% focused on what I'm saying. But then there are moments like when you're in a packed club and the beat to this song drops and it's just enormous, like a spiritual experience, and I have to reconsider.

Careful listeners may notice that I re-recorded this entire song just to swap out "illegal immigrants" for "undocumented workers," because we all should be more intentional with our words.

Produced by Big Cats
Original version appeared on "An Unwelcome Guest," though the version here is a new recording with a few new lyrics swapped in.

YOU SAY MILLIONAIRE LIKE IT'S A GOOD THING
This is the newest song included here, written in early 2014 and unavailable anywhere but on this sampler. Moving forward, I'm really interested in exploring this idea of extreme wealth as a legitimate moral and ethical failing. This song is pretty blunt about it, but I think there's a lot of territory to mine there.

I wanted to deliver my verses here kind of dead-eyed and sleepily and let the beat do the heavy lifting. The hypnotic effect may not work for everyone, but my hope is that it highlights the substance of the song.

Produced by Ganzobean
Appeared on "A Love Song, A Death Rattle, A Battle Cry"

RIVERBED
Another brand new song; another recurring theme in all of my work: death. I talk about death a lot. Sometimes it's subtle or in the background, and sometimes it's "Riverbed," which is just everything I want to say about the concept of death in 32 bars.

Produced by Ganzobean
Appeared on "A Love Song, A Death Rattle, A Battle Cry"

WHOSE PLANET? OUR PLANET
Just about every album I've released has had a token shit-talking rap song. As much as I've built my career around challenging substance, poetic writing and original concepts, I'm still a sucker for some good, old-fashioned flexing. That's part of hip hop culture, and it's just fun to do too.

For me, it's also important to do songs like this in order to push back against the pigeon-holing that inevitably befalls all of us. I love being known as an artist who has meaningful things to say and says them in a poetic way. However, there's a greedy part of me, deep down, who also wants to be known as an excellent technical MC, an excellent punchline MC, a funny MC, etc. Competition is part of the culture, and as problematic as that is for some people, I can definitely see the upside.

Produced by Rube
Additional words/vocals by deM atlaS
Appeared on "Sifu Hotman: Embrace the Sun"

THE FOURTH WALL

This is the third version of this song, and I think I finally got it right, thanks to a summery beat from Katrah-Quey and guest vocals from Lydia Liza of Bomba de Luz. I wrote the hook, but Lydia wrote her bridge part, in the studio. The last verse here is an homage to "Thought Process" when the beat fades out and Andre keeps rapping over the handclaps.

I ended up working with Katrah-Quey for the entirety of my latest album, "Post-Post-Race," and it was a great experience. That album is something very different, and I'm proud of it. As for Lydia—she's one of the most talented people I know, and I can't wait to make more music with her in the future.

Produced by Katrah-Quey
Additional words/vocals by Lydia Liza

THE HERO

My whole career is a kind of concept album. Almost all of my poems and songs explore the idea of power—where it comes from, how it's abused, how it can be focused, etc. This song is one of the most direct examples of that. I just wanted to take that age-old question of "what would you do if you had superpowers?" and do something different with it.

Aside from the message, this song is also one of many straight-up narrative tracks in my arsenal. Storytelling in hip hop is a tradition, and it's one that I don't want to see go away.

Finally, this is also one of a number of superhero-focused songs that I've written (see also: "No Capes" and "Greater Shout"). I don't think I have anything revelatory to say about superhero mythology; it's been covered so exhaustively elsewhere; but I do think that recontextualizing those ideas in rap songs breathes a little more life into them. While I find straight-up "nerd-core" hip hop to be sometimes... problematic, I do think that sci-fi/comic book ideas are fertile ground for exploring the kinds of ideas in this song.

Produced by Big Cats
Appeared on "Start a Fire" and "Don't Be Nice"

BREAK
This might be the strongest all-around song on what is definitely my strongest all-around album, "You Better Weaponize." The thing is, almost all of the credit has to go to Kristoff, who wrote his verse, the hook, and the back-and-forth intro, as well as Big Cats, who made a gorgeous beat.

My challenge was to write my verses around Kristoff's, to really focus on a concrete narrative that could anchor his stream-of-consciousness style in a way that made both of us shine. One of the reasons I love working with artists like Kristoff, Joe Horton, and Crescent Moon is how different our approaches to writing are. I think that when the balance is struck properly, the effect is really powerful.

The first verse here is brand new, and doesn't appear on the original version of this song. There are also a handful of changes in the text (and in the live performance of this) that aren't reflected in this recording; I'm trying to remove ableist language from my vocabulary.

Produced by Big Cats
Additional words/vocals by Kristoff Krane
Appeared on "You Better Weaponize"

LIGHTNING
By the time this book comes out, Chastity will probably be a huge star so I don't need to say much about her. She's endlessly inspiring. She wrote the outro here and it's such a huge release for a song that basically just builds for three minutes.

The idea of embracing negative energy/emotions rather than suppressing them is a huge recurring theme in my work. It's also a pretty huge recurring theme in my life.

Beyond that, I think the key line in this song is "there is no progress without struggle" (hat-tip to Frederick Douglass). I have the enormous privilege of being paid to travel around the country and talk to young people. If there is ONE message I want to make sure I can convey, it is the fundamental importance of people working together to create change. I want to help cultivate a culture of organizing, as opposed to a culture of "voting for the right person" or "hoping things inevitably get better."

That's maybe a secondary message in this particular song, but it's a central message in my work at the macro level.

Produced by Big Cats
Additional words/vocals by Chastity Brown
Appeared on "You Better Weaponize"

DRAGONS
This is one of those songs where certain lines in the verses make me cringe (just in the sense that they were written with the rhyme in mind moreso than the content), but it's easily the best hook I ever wrote so I had to include it on this sampler.

For an artist who is almost always talked about as being a "political rapper," I've written a lot of love songs. I think that juxtaposition is important—love songs can be political, and political songs can be about love... and probably should be.

The original version was produced by Big Cats and appeared at the climactic moment of our concept album "An Unwelcome Guest," but I wanted to include this new remix on the sampler as a change of pace.

Produced by New Convert
Appeared on "A Love Song, A Death Rattle, A Battle Cry"

A PRAGMATIST'S GUIDE TO REVOLUTION
The sampler version of this song is a mashup of three different tracks, though I think Graham's beat really masks that and turns it into a powerful song on its own. It's a bit long to perform live, but sometimes I do anyway just for that incredible outro that Graham produced.
This song is also an intentional break from the conceptuality that dominates most of my work. Its message is very straightforward, and there aren't a ton of big overarching metaphors or anything.

I don't think either approach is better or worse; just two different tools.

If I can spread any message to the people who pay attention to me, it's that change comes from people working together. It's not magic, it's not impossible, and it's not "too big to imagine." Join an organization. Dive in. Get to work. That's how people have made things better for thousands of years. Overthinking can be as dangerous as underthinking when a sense of urgency is needed.

Produced by Graham O'Brien
"A Pragmatist's Guide to Revolution" and "Until There's Nothing Left"
appeared on "You Better Weaponize"
"11020200" appeared on "Start a Fire"

SPIRIT BOMB
This is the oldest song included in this mix. I wrote this when I was like 19 or something, and you can probably tell. But I had to include it here due to See More's beat, which is some beautiful hip hop Princess Mononoke stuff. See More Perspective is one of my long-time collaborators, and he's done so much great work over the years. Check him out.

While it may be a little on the nose here, I still like the idea of a love song being a vessel for a message that isn't about romantic/ relationship love at all. Love songs are such a deeply-rooted part of our culture; I think there's a lot of potential to subvert and play with them. That's what the whole EP "A Loud Heart" does, as well as this song.

Produced by See More Perspective
Appeared on "Return to Guante's Haunted Studio Apartment"

ONE OF THESE MORNINGS
Another song about death, though I don't think most people interpret it like that. The hook comes from the original version of this song, where producer G-force sampled "Summertime." The remix loses the sample, but gains some urgency.

A lot of my songs tend to be a little more blunt, in terms of their messaging, when compared to my poems. I want to make sure that my point gets across not just for the kid listening five times in headphones at home, but for the kid at the live show who only has one shot to catch the ideas as well. This song, however, I think strikes a balance that some of my other songs don't-- certain lines are very direct, but the overall thesis statement of the song is something deeper.

Produced by Big Cats
Original version appeared on "Start a Fire," though the version included here is a new recording with a few new lyrics swapped in.

THIS IS THE OPPOSITE OF A SUICIDE NOTE
Graham recorded and mixed a lot of my songs, especially the newer ones, and we've only just begun collaborating musically. He's the drummer in No Bird Sing, as well as the musical mastermind behind a handful of other bands and projects, and really just another one of the most talented people I know.

This is another entry in my series of "long verse, no hook" songs. That's a songwriting challenge that I love, and it also allows producers to build a lot of dynamism into their beats.

Produced by Graham O'Brien
Appeared on "A Love Song, A Death Rattle, A Battle Cry"

REVOLVER
On a poetic level, I think this is the best song I ever wrote. And Claire's hook and bridge are just heartbreaking. This might also be the straight-up prettiest song I've ever been part of. Honorable mention to "Asterisk," which I wanted to include on the sampler too but ran out of room.

This track and the next one are both about the scope of struggle, and about the relationship between micro and macro. Progress isn't always a single brushstroke of a single moment; it's often a million tiny acts, separated by time, place, and intention, building up to something more.

Guitar and additional words/vocals by Claire de Lune
Cello by Renee Klitzke
Appeared on "A Loud Heart"

A PRAGMATIST'S GUIDE TO FAITH
I've always separated my music from my spoken word stuff, but this piece (along with "Lightning" and a few others) really represents my starting to break down some of those walls. I wrote this as a song, but never recorded it over a beat. Maybe it's a song, a capella; maybe it's a poem that rhymes, I don't know. But I like how it feels when I'm performing it. I think a lot of my future work is going to be in this vein.

With this piece, I wanted to talk about how even though bad things like racism, sexism, and inequality are these giant institutions deeply rooted in our history, I think good things like resistance and hope are also giant institutions deeply rooted in our history. Whenever we act on our principles, we're taking part in a struggle that is larger than us, and larger than our generation.

There is a lot of responsibility that comes from that, and maybe some pressure. But there is also strength that can be drawn from that. Like a lot of my work, this is a reminder to myself as much as it is a message for anyone else out there.

Recorded live at the 2014 Be Heard MN Youth Poetry Slam Finals
Appeared on "A Love Song, A Death Rattle, A Battle Cry"

ESSAYS AND OTHER WRITING

Most of these essays and op-eds have appeared online in some form or another over the past couple of years, but part of the power of a book is being able to juxtapose them, especially in the context of some of the poems and songs in the previous sections.

During the process of putting this book together, however, this was the section that made me the most nervous. Over the past few years, I've tried to be very intentional with my writing. Especially when writing about social justice issues, I think it's vital that I acknowledge my own positionality and speak up in a way that isn't speaking over others. In some ways, this is easier to do online, where you can embed links to other people's work, and create space for dialogue, critique, and questioning. Seeing these essays *in a book* is a bit of a trip for me, since most of them were written less as "my definitive take on a subject for all eternity" and more as "a few thoughts to transmit to the people who like my Facebook page, in the hopes of sparking some dialogue."

Along those lines, I also think a lot about what audiences I have access to, and what I might have to offer the larger conversation. Part of my nervousness about this section is related to the idea that most of these pieces were written for an online audience who might have never engaged with these topics before, or are actively resistant to them, whereas the people who buy this book (thanks!) might already *get* everything in here, or even be able to critique it from deeper or more radical perspectives.

And that's cool. While all of these things have been on my mind, I am again erring on the side of transparency-into-the-process. I'm a very different writer today than I was even a year or two ago, when most of these essays were written—but that's always going to be true. My hope is that there is some value in the substance of this writing, but also in being able to see my own process and journey. Since there's no comment system in a book, feel free to disagree and call me names with a red pen instead.

TEN THINGS EVERYONE SHOULD KNOW ABOUT HIP HOP

I've been an MC for about ten years. I don't say that to position myself as any kind of scholarly hip hop expert; I'm not. I'm a practitioner. And as a practitioner, I've noticed that there are a few fairly basic things that a whole lot of people seem to regularly get wrong about hip hop—at conferences, in classes, in online debates and just in conversation. So what follows are ten simple—but important—things that I wish everyone knew about hip hop.

1. Hip Hop is Big
The rap music that you hear on the radio or see on TV is less than 1% of what is actually being made in the world. To dismiss all hip hop based on that kind of superficial exposure is like saying "film is a worthless art form" after seeing all of the Transformers movies and nothing else.

2. Hip Hop is Diverse and Dynamic
Once you acknowledge that hip hop is bigger than the half-dozen artists they play on the radio over and over again, you can begin to appreciate the vast stylistic diversity present in the music. While there are a number of commonly shared elements (rhymes, verse/chorus structures, drums, etc.) individual artists can and do have wildly different approaches to the form in terms of style, subject matter, voice, and delivery. The complex, ever-shifting geography of hip hop's many subcultures, undercurrents and call-and-response aesthetic debates is one of its greatest strengths.

3. Hip Hop is Global
Every city in the U.S. has a hip hop scene. It's not just New York, and it's not just major population centers. Even suburbs and smaller rural communities often have one or two kids who rap, or at the very least take part in the culture in some way. On top of that, just about

every country in the world has a hip hop scene, with MCs rapping in many different languages and dialects, b-boy and b-girl communities sprouting up all over the world, and hip hop as a major driver of youth culture just about everywhere on the planet.

4. There is a Difference Between "Hip Hop" and "Rap" But It's Probably Not What You Think

Individuals will often try to differentiate between the two terms based on content/quality (like *rappers just rap while hip hop MCs represent for the culture*), but a less subjective definition is this: "Rap" is the physical act of rapping, of speaking lyrics over beats. "Hip hop" is the larger culture that includes rapping, but also includes many other elements, traditions, and practices.

5. Hip Hop Isn't Just Rap Music

The traditional four elements of hip hop are DJing, MCing, graffiti, and b-boy/b-girl dance. KRS-ONE and others have identified additional elements that are sometimes thrown into the conversation: vocal percussion and beatboxing, design & fashion, knowledge, entrepreneurialism, slang and language, music production, and more. I know hip hop photographers, hip hop educators, hip hop activists, hip hop playwrights, etc. It helps to think about hip hop as this impressionistic landscape, not just as "rap music." It's much bigger than that.

6. While Practitioners Today Come from Many Different Backgrounds, Hip Hop is Part of Black American Musical Tradition

Hip hop was born out of the Black and brown struggle in the Bronx of the 1970s, and is very much a piece of African-American musical tradition (read: hip hop is Black music). But practitioners of the art today include representatives from every community—every racial/ethnic group, gender, sexual orientation, immigrant status, nationality, class background, geographic origin and any other marker of identity.

Some see this as another example of Black art being co-opted; some see this as a truly multicultural art form capable of transcending borders. Some see it as both.

7. Hip hop is Not Inherently Violent, Sexist or Homophobic

To be clear, I'm not saying that there isn't quite a bit of violence, sexism and homophobia in rap lyrics. But the key word here is "inherently." To re-use the film metaphor, there's a whole lot of violence, sexism and homophobia in Hollywood too, but that doesn't mean that film is an inherently debased medium, or that there aren't thousands upon thousands of examples (indeed—the overwhelming majority) of movies that break from that trend.

8. There May Be a Difference Between "Mainstream" and "Underground" But It's Probably Not What You Think

While it's convenient rhetoric to state that independent, underground hip hop is all revolution and consciousness and eating vegetables, while mainstream hip hop is all guns, cars and pimps, that's wildly oversimplified. There are plenty of underground MCs saying ignorant or otherwise meaningless things, and plenty of famous MCs who are pushing boundaries in terms of both style and substance.

Clearly, an artist with major label backing and a multi-million dollar promotional budget will have a different approach than a kid making beats in his basement, but for the most part, "Mainstream vs. Underground" is a false binary that simplifies the culture in a way that makes it easier to not authentically engage with the art itself.

9. Hip Hop History is Complex, Fascinating, and Above All, Important

If you want to better grasp ideas like benign neglect, gentrification, institutional racism, the relationship between artistic expression and American capitalism, or the power of popular resistance to oppression, read Jeff Chang's "Can't Stop, Won't Stop," the best hip hop history book I've come across. There are a lot of good books about hip hop out there, but I'd recommend starting with that one.

10. Hip Hop is Beautiful

I know, this one is subjective. But the older I get, the more I move away from the "here are the three artists I like so I'm going to compare everyone else to them!" framework. Instead, it's really about active listening and critical thinking. There is something to appreciate and something to critique in every song, every album, every artist. And when you do that, when you take the time and energy to actually engage with the culture (even if you're not actively part of the culture) it's indescribably rewarding.

HIP HOP: A PANEL DISCUSSION

Cast:

- Colin Pennyworth, 20, hipster music journalist
- Young Lil', 25, hip hop artist
- Prof. Alastair Cheffordshire, 67, anthropology professor
- Jamie "Jaymix" Wester, 34, hip hop activist
- Guante, 27, Midwest nobody
- Moderator Sarah Mulligan, 44, local news personality

(The scene: a full auditorium at the local university's student union. Our panelists are on a stage behind a table. The moderator stands at a podium to the right. The audience is composed primarily of college students, but a few younger and older faces pepper the crowd as well. Four white kids are cyphering in the back).

Mulligan: I'd like to welcome all of our panelists. So as you all know, we're here today to talk about hip hop. We've got about half an hour, which should be more than enough time. So the first question: Nas *(pronounced "Nass")* had an album out a few years ago called "Hip Hop Is Dead." Is hip hop dead?

Wester: I'll jump right in and say, as KRS-ONE once told me, HIP HOP isn't dead. HIP HOP lives in the projects called your heart. HIP HOP goes to work every day putting food on your table. See, there's HIP HOP and then there's HIP HOP, and...

Young Lil' *(interrupting)*: Nah mean, Nas is a real smart dude. No homo. He charts well. I mean, people in the hood ain't tryin' to hear that book shit, but he still sells records. And that beef...

Pennyworth *(interrupting)*: Nas is just an out of touch New York rapper who doesn't understand what the streets want. See, the South is on top now. Maybe if he quit being an elitist hack and wrote a few dozen songs about selling crack, he'd be singing a different tune. I had a sit-down with Jeezy the other day, and he told me...

Cheffordshire (*interrupting*): I'm afraid I'll have to disagree with you there old boy. Like I say in my new book, Nas is a modern-day street prophet, a GRIOT, if you will, who translates ancient African folktales into a thoroughly postmodern gumbo that speaks directly to the blues experience. When he says that hip hop is dead, he is, quite obviously, alluding directly to OSIRIS, the Egyptian god of the dead. To die is to transcend, to become more-than, and Nas is quite simply following in the footsteps of Public Enemy as he...

Mulligan (*interrupting*): Mr. Guante, you've been rather quiet. Do you think hip hop is dead?

Guante: Um... no? I think that's kind of an oversimplification. Do you mean hip hop as a global culture? Hip hop as art? Hip hop as a commodity? Hip hop as a force on the pop charts? These are all very different. Really, what does that question even mean? I think...

Mulligan (*interrupting*) Well since you don't understand the question, let's move on. Backtracking a little, what IS hip hop?

Wester (*eyes lighting up*): HIP HOP IS A CULTURE COMPOSED OF 37 ELEMENTS: b-boying, graffiti, DJing, MCing, beatboxing, street knowledge, street entrepreneurialism, street app design, street manicure/pedicure, breakfast cereal, beat production, martial arts movies, street upholstery...

Pennyworth (*interrupting*): Here we go again with that hip hop culture shit. I was on the phone with Pusha T of the Clipse the other day and he told me...

Young Lil' (*interrupting*): Hip hop is like, it's like, crazy, man. It's like, a voice. Like, I'm Martin Luther King or Malcolm X or some shit... no homo.

Cheffordshire: Yes! Precisely, my dear boy. Hip hop is the united battlecry of the African-American proletariat, awakening from its slumber to reclaim its objective identity. It is Athena, bursting fully formed from the noble skull of Zeus. Hip Hop creates subjective spaces wherein objective reality can...

Mulligan (*interrupting*): But what about the sexism? Isn't there a lot of sexism in hip hop?

Young Lil''s manager (*suddenly appearing behind the panel*): Can I just jump in here for a minute? See, hip hop ain't sexist; AMERICA is sexist. Hip hop is just reflecting that reality.

Young Lil': Yeah and also, some bitches ARE bitches.

Young Lil''s manager: Exactly. My man here is a ghetto reporter, showing middle America the objective facts about the 'hood. You all should be thanking him for performing a valuable public service! Guante: Your breakthrough single was called "Stomp a Ho Out (Over Nothing)!" Yeah, America is sexist, but there comes a point when we as artists need to...

Wester (*interrupting*): HAVE YOU GUYS EVER HEARD OF COMMON? OR MOS DEF? OR TALIB KWELI? THOSE GUYS ARE GREAT AND THEY RESPECT WOMEN AND TALK ABOUT REAL ISSUES. IT'S NOT ALL GUNS, HOS AND CARS. YOU SHOULD CHECK OUT THE ROOTS' NEW ALBUM.

Pennyworth (*rolling eyes*): Those are all old men who only sell records to white hippies. I may be from Maine, but I know that the streets don't want to be preached to. Music should be devoid of social commentary because that shit is preachy. TI and Lil' Wayne might be sexist, sure, but that's real. And the beats are transcendent, slathering mountains of sticky sweet boombap with robo-sexy future synths and rumbling, neck-biting basslines. I had sushi with Ghostface the other day, and he told me...

Mulligan (*interrupting*): Don Imus. How 'bout that?

Young Lil"'s manager: He's a hater. He just hates. It's all just hate, man.

Cheffordshire: What Mr. Imus fails to grasp is that neo-liberalism has created a kind of post-traumatic psychic shock in the African-American collective cultural consciousness. By invoking the terms he did, Imus has, in a sense, awakened the Cyclops, and now even the softest wool will serve as poor protection against the rage of the injured beast.

(pause... not in, like, a homophobic "pause" kind of way, but an actual pause)

Guante: The Don Imus incident was four years ago! Are we going to talk about East Coast vs. West Coast beef next?

Mulligan: How about violence. Isn't there a war going on between the East Coast and the West Coast? Is hip hop inherently violent?

Young Lil"'s manager: No. It's not. Simple as that. It's fantasy. My man here is a poet, a master storyteller. We don't get mad at Arnold for making "Terminator." We make him the governor of goddamn California. My man here is just telling highly detailed, poetic stories.

Guante: But didn't you just say that Young Lil' was a "ghetto reporter, showing middle America objective facts?"

Pennyworth: You're obviously one of those elitists who thinks all hip hop should be boring piano loops and songs that say something. Why can't you just respect Young Lil"'s body of work? I gave his last album, "I Sell Crack (You Just Die)," a 7.4 out of 10, the highest rating I've ever given anything. It was a masterpiece of dark, urban paranoia, mixing crackling high hats, shabble-tastic synth grooves and multilayered, techno-organic vocalizationals. Meeting him reminded me of meeting Mobb Deep's Prodigy for the first time back in...

Wester: COMMON NEVER RAPS ABOUT SHOOTING PEOPLE. HE'S MORE LIKE A POET. MOS DEF MADE A SONG ABOUT CONSERVING WATER! TALIB KWELI! DID YOU KNOW THAT "EMCEE" IS AN ACRONYM FOR "EVERYONE MAKES CULTURE EVOLVE ETERNALLY?"

Young Lil': I will shoot you though. Just so we're clear.

Mulligan: Let's take some questions from the audience. You there.

Dirty Backpacker: Hey duuudes, I just wanted to say that I think Jedi Mind Tricks is frickin' dope. What do you duuudes think?

(Pennyworth makes "jerking-off" motion with his hands, the rest of the panel stays quiet.)

Mulligan: Okay next question. You there.

Obvious College Student: I'm writing a paper on 2pac and Black Nationalism and I was wondering if you guys had any thoughts on... that.

Cheffordshire: In my new book, I say that Tupac Amaru Shakur was a modern day Rumi, perhaps mixed with Alexander Pope and Basho. His words can be endlessly analyzed because he directly channeled the oral traditions of...

Young Lil' *(interrupting)*: 'Pac was real, you know. He sold a lot of records. I like that song about his mother because I love my mama too. No homo.

Mulligan: I think we'll take one last question. How about you in the back?

Little Kid: Isn't it a bit presumptuous to think you can cover all of hip hop in a half-hour panel discussion? I mean, this audience is composed of people with different levels of prior understanding, different life experiences, and different ways of interacting with the culture. Hip hop is an enormous, complex global culture that is fluid and ever-evolving, yet we still talk about it like it's some New York fad. Wasn't this whole farce just a meaningless exercise in intellectual masturbation? Don't half-assed discussions like this, whether at a conference or on cable news, always just undergird whatever assumptions people already have about hip hop, good or bad?

Mulligan: No. Okay now on to the closing statements. Professor, would you like to begin?

Cheffordshire: Oh hip hop, thou many-headed hydra, wherefore shall we find thee? In my new book, I write that Chuck D. of Public Enemy, while pioneering a kind of neo-romantic poststructuralist er er ER er ER ER rhythm, was in fact alluding to—and paying tribute to—his intellectual forebears, the guild poets of the Russian Revolution. And this is where we find hip hop today, at a crossroads. The Scylla of postmodernism on one side, the Charybdis of Marxist determinism on the other, the good ship hip hop must sail carefully, the winds of revolution in her sails, always forward, always backward.

Young Lil"s manager: And I would just add on to that: haters hate. That's all it really is. Like, some groups have called my man here homophobic. He ain't homophobic. AMERICA is homophobic.

Young Lil': And besides, I ain't AFRAID of gays, I just don't like to be around them, hear their voices or read about them in magazines.

Young Lil"s manager: Exactly. My man here is a PROPHET. He's like a cross between 2pac and Biggie, but with that Southern flavor that's hot right now. Make sure you cop that new album.

Pennyworth: Three Six Mafia's zombieflutter chipmunk soul sound, combined with their stubbly, Goodburger basslines, ghetto dilapidated kicks and pure bricktop syrupy freneticism are really the only hope this middling genre has left. I split a muffin with Juicy J the other day, and he...

Wester (*interrupting*): I THINK THAT IN THE NEXT TWO YEARS, MOS DEF, TALIB KWELI, COMMON AND THE ROOTS ARE GOING TO DO AN ALBUM TOGETHER AND IT WILL SPARK A WORLDWIDE REVOLUTION OF HEALING AND REVOLUTION AND CONSCIOUSNESS. THEIR BRILLIANT POETRY WILL FREE ALL POLITICAL PRISONERS, GIVE BREAD TO THE HUNGRY AND EDUCATE OUR CHILDREN.

Mulligan: Mr. Guante?

Guante: O...K... I guess if I can say anything about this ridiculous fiasco, it'd be that...

Mulligan (*interrupting*): I'm gonna have to cut you off there. Sorry, we're out of time. I'd like to thank all our panelists, the audience, and the conference organizers. Drive safely.

HE IS WHATEVER WE SAY HE IS: A ONE-ACT PLAY ON EMINEM, HIP HOP AESTHETICS, AND FAME

From *Eminem and Rap, Poetry, Race: Essays* © 2014 Edited by Scott F. Parker by permission of McFarland & Company, Inc., Box 611, Jefferson NC 28640. www.mcfarlandpub.com

Cast:

- Hater Jones, 21, hater
- Professor Baker, 56, Black Studies professor
- Colin Pennyworth, 26, hipster music journalist
- Stanley Johnson, 19, Eminem fan
- Eddie Kay, 22, hip hop head

(The scene: the cafeteria at a community college—late afternoon, nearly all of the lunch traffic has passed; Professor Baker and Colin Pennyworth walk by, glancing over to a lunch table at a freestyle cypher in progress).

Hater Jones: *(beatboxing)*

Eddie Kay: *(rapping, in progress):* ...you know the spit stay vicious, the kid is, flippin' by the minute / g'd up like G-Dep spittin' "let's get it."

Stanley Johnson: *(rapping):* Yeah, let's get it, you better call the medics / I leave your abdomen sliced open with intestines / fallin' out, callin' out all these fake lames / usin' your appendix as a hand grenade . . . *(sees Baker and Pennyworth and stops)* You wanna join the cypher?

Colin Pennyworth: *(laughs)* No, no. I was just interviewing the professor here for an article I'm writing about hip hop. He said he sees you three in here almost every day and thinks you might be good interview subjects too.

Eddie Kay: Oh yeah? What's the article about?

Colin Pennyworth: It's mostly about the record industry, and how people aren't really buying CDs any more. The timely element is that it'll be published right around the time Eminem's new album drops, and I'm kind of using that as a lens through which we can—

Hater Jones: (*loudly interrupting*) Ayo, does the universe really need another article about Eminem?

Professor Baker: (*chuckles*)

Colin Pennyworth: Why do you say that?

Stanley Johnson: Because he's a *hater*, that's why.

Hater Jones: Nah, nah. I'm just the only one left who can see that the emperor ain't got no clothes on. I just see through the shtick. I'm not gonna say he's not talented, but I *am* gonna say he started out as overrated and devolved into audio vomit faster than a crappy Yelawolf double-time verse; he's been coasting ever since "Lose Yourself" dropped. Now he's all weird voices and melodramatic pop bullshit, and I just cannot fathom why people keep buying his records and writing articles about him.

Stanley Johnson (*rolls eyes*): Maybe it's because he's the best songwriter in hip hop? Maybe it's because he writes songs that show his actual emotions and isn't just talking about bitches and cars and money? Maybe it's because he's a flat-out better rapper than anyone else ever? Maybe it's because the level of thought he puts into—

Professor Baker: Or maybe it's because he's white? Let's not ignore the elephant in the room here.

Stanley Johnson: So why isn't Cage world famous? Or Eyedea? Or Asher Roth? Race has nothing to do with it.

Eddie Kay: Whoa there, fam. Of course race has something to do with it. But in his defense, you also can't deny Em's pure technical ability. I mean, artists like Pharaohe Monch and Tech N9ne and them have been doing microphone acrobatics for years, but there's not really anyone out there who sounds like Em, who makes it look so effortless. Even on his later stuff, which I agree has its problems, he's out-rhyming the devil in there, just mad syllable chains and mind-blowing flow patterns and all that.

Professor Baker: But you said it yourself—other artists, Black artists, have been doing what he does for years. He jumps in with his own amateur take on something someone else built and is propped up as the messiah. He sells a whitewashed version of Black culture to white children, and in the process becomes the most celebrated and successful hip hop artist in history. The Elvis comparison may be an easy one, but it's only easy because it's so accurate.

Hater Jones: Exactly. Eminem makes music for white trash pre-teens who think fart jokes are hilarious and drugs are edgy. It's some lowest-common-denominator shit, and that will always make you famous in America.

Stanley Johnson: (*scoffs*) Did either of you ever even listen to "Stan," or "Cleanin' Out My Closet," or "Hailie's Song," or "Love the Way You Lie," or—

Hater Jones (*interrupting*): Oh you mean the song where he got Rihanna to sing a hook about refusing to leave an abusive relationship? Yeah, that's deep, man.

Stanley Johnson: It *is* deep. The song is about breaking the cycle, about how hard it is to—

Hater Jones: He's just chasing clicks, homie. Trying to remain relevant because everybody knows his skills just ain't there no more. Maybe that's why he SHOUTS all his LYRICS now—he's getting desperate, on some "I'M NOT AFRAID"—

Eddie Kay: *(laughing)* What about you, Mr. Music Writer? What do you think about Eminem?

Colin Pennyworth: I don't know. I guess for me, it's about angles. You can always find something to say about him. Yeah, you can write about the novelty of a white rapper, but you can also write about the Dr. Dre cosign, or the shockingly offensive lyrics, or the untouchable skillset, or all the high-profile beefs. For a music writer, he's really the gift that keeps on giving.

Eddie Kay: And that's the problem for me. Like I said, I like Em; I think he has crazy talent. But who out there is actually writing about talent? Y'all pick up some narrative or angle and run with it, but no one seems to care about the actual music any more.

Hater Jones: Exactly. It's funny that Em beefed with Canibus, because if Eminem were Black, he'd *be* Canibus. Another technically proficient weirdo rapper. "But he's white, and Dr. Dre likes him, so here's your GOAT," says the media.

Professor Baker: "Here's your goat?"

Eddie Kay: Greatest of All Time. And for the record, I think he's in the conversation, extracurriculars aside. Just on pure skills alone. Top ten at least, maybe cracking the top five—

Stanley Johnson: Man, he *is* the conversation. Who else is even on that same plane of existence? You can really name five MCs better than Em?

(all at once):
Eddie Kay: Rakim, Jay, Big L, Big Pun, Nas.
Hater Jones: Jay, Biggie, Pac, KRS, Andre from Outkast.
Professor Baker: Chuck D, Rakim, 2Pac, KRS-One, Nas.

Stanley Johnson: You're all crazy. Ain't none of them seeing Em, bar for bar.

Colin Pennyworth: As someone who isn't as well versed in rap, I'm inclined to agree. Just to my ears, he's doing something that's wildly different. Listening to some of these old-school guys these days is like watching a black-and-white TV after visiting the IMAX theater.

Professor Baker: But there it is. "As someone who isn't as well-versed in rap." You're Mathers' target audience. He appropriates Black culture, performs his rhymes without the polyrhythmic "swing" of his more culturally attuned peers, subverts and ridicules Black masculinity, and all but spits on hip hop's history as a tool of uplift for Black and brown peoples, all while—

Eddie Kay: Hey, hey now. A tool of uplift? You ever actually listen to the lyrics to "Rapper's Delight?" Or any old-school shit beyond "The Message" and "The Breaks?" My dad is from NY and he has a box full of tapes from that era; I've listened to them all. Rap used to be about having fun and showing off your skills. Sure, the existence of the art itself may have been implicitly political and may have served as a tool of uplift, but I think it's a misrepresentation of history to imply that this was all some conscious master plan. In that sense, I think Em is paying homage to the culture's origins, even if I don't agree with his sexism or homophobia or shock-for-shock's-sake lyrics, he's killing it with the flows. He's showcasing his talent. He's having fun making words rhyme, and I respect that.

Hater Jones: But is that enough? I mean, it rips me up inside to admit this, but yeah, the kid can spit. But so can Myka 9. So can Pharaohe. So can Gift of Gab. So can a million other MCs none of us have ever heard of. Em may have talent, but he's never been famous because of his talent, let's be honest.

Colin Pennyworth: So why is he so famous?

Hater Jones: Because people like you keep shoving him down our throats instead of writing about any of the million other talented MCs in this country.

Colin Pennyworth: (*taken aback*) . . . but, I mean, I'm just giving our readers what they want. He's famous because people like him—that's what talent is, right? Making music that people like? It's not like we've picked some nerdy underdog white backpacker super-scientifical MC to get everyone to jump on *his* bandwagon. It's not my fault he's white, and even my Black friends think . . .

Eddie Kay: (*interrupting*) Okay, okay, we get it, relax. Let me answer your question another way. Let's think back to when the *Slim Shady LP* dropped. It was 1999, post-Telecommunications Act, when mainstream hip hop was at its most hedonistically blinged-out and capitalistic and underground hip hop was at its most grimy and challenging. You got Nelly, Ja Rule, DMX, and Jay-Z on one side, and then you got the Roots, Mos Def, Company Flow, and dead prez on the other. And then you turn on the TV and it's the video for "My Name Is." And this shit just didn't make any sense. It didn't really belong anywhere. This wasn't just a white guy rapping. It wasn't just a white guy rapping well. It wasn't just a white guy rapping well with Dr. Dre in his video. That song was *weird*. To this day, "My Name Is" is a weird-ass song that doesn't sound like anything else out there. It got play on alternative rock stations—

Professor Baker: (*coughing*) WHITENESS!

Eddie Kay: Yeah, you're right, but it's not *just* about whiteness. In the same way that it's not *just* about talent. Either of those things may be the main ingredient in a given context, but you can't make chili with nothing but beans. That song—and that album—blew up because of its novelty. And I mean novelty not like a gimmick, like "look at this whiteboy with the funny voice rapping about crazy shit," but as in something novel, something new and different and, for a lot of people, refreshing. And yeah, he can spit too, which doesn't hurt.

Hater Jones: It just doesn't seem fair to me that he gets so much attention for being quote-unquote "novel." Like I said, lots of rappers are talented. And lots of rappers are novel. These days, lots of rappers are white. Maybe it's because he's all three, I don't know; right place at the right time with the right skin tone kind of thing. It's still some bullshit. I get that he has some talent, but how people can just look right past his godawful beat selection, laughably wack singing hooks, emo-ass lyrics, tough-guy posturing, and all that misogyny and homophobia.

Professor Baker: You know, I hate to be the old man saying the same thing over and over, but that's textbook white privilege. In this culture, white celebrities are readily forgiven for all but the worst offenses. We look the other way. A white athlete, musician, actor, or politician can do everything wrong and still succeed. The world is set up for them to succeed. Mathers may be talented; I don't know. I don't think he is at all. But like Mr. Jones pointed out—that talent has its limits, yet public praise for it seemingly does not.

Stanley Johnson: *But he's the best rapper ever!* That's basically an objective *fact!*

Eddie Kay: (*laughing*) Objective? How is that an objective fact?

Stanley Johnson: Look. It's math. You can break down any MC into some combination of flows, content, songwriting, voice and relevance. You guys do it all the time. It's why Boots Riley is objectively better than Waka Flocka. Waka may be more relevant, but loses out in all the other categories.

Hater Jones: I mean, voice would be a tossup.

Stanley Johnson: Sure, whatever. But when you look at Eminem, he gets a ten out of ten in all five categories. He's an omega-level MC. The only one, too. You just can't argue with that.

Professor Baker: Dear boy, I think I could argue with that. Your categories themselves are subjective, and furthermore, it seems to me that one category missing from your framework is cultural foundation. Is it not true that artists, especially artists representing—indeed embodying—the white supremacist-capitalist-hetero-patriarchy, should be held accountable to the culture from which they purloin their very livelihoods?

Stanley Johnson: (*thinks for a moment*) You just don't like him because he's white! You teach a class on hip hop and you don't even listen to any hip hop after 1995!

Professor Baker: And you only like him because he is white! You weren't even born in 1995 and know nothing about the culture's history!

Hater Jones: (*to Pennyworth*) See what it's like to try to have a critical conversation about this dude?

Eddie Kay: (*laughs*) And that's key, right? I feel like most people aren't interested in having any kind of critical conversation. It's either Em is the GOAT and beyond reproach or Em is an overrated culture vulture. But hip hop has never been that simple. He's both. He's neither. On some Zen shit, you have to hold both realities in your mind at the same time. If you want to really talk about Eminem—or hip hop in general for that matter—you have to grapple with complication, you have to engage in the kind of dialogue that maybe doesn't fit into a one-line thesis statement, or a 300-word album review, or a punch line. Instead of asking pointless, abstract questions like "Do white people belong in hip hop?" let's ask "What is the responsibility of white people in hip hop to the culture?" Instead of asking "Is Eminem the best ever?" let's have more conversations about hip hop aesthetics and what makes someone "good" or "bad." Instead of writing another pretentious-ass sociology paper with a long-ass title bifurcated by a colon, let's try to, I don't know, actually listen to the music, go to some local rap shows, and develop a real relationship with the culture. In the end, I don't even care about Eminem; but if he can be a gateway for people to start to really understand hip hop as the vibrant, growing, beautiful culture that it is, let's have that conversation. Let's keep it moving.

Colin Pennyworth: ...Right. Sooooo, back to my article, what do you guys think about Macklemore?

Hater Jones, Stanley Johnson, Eddie Kay (*simultaneously*): We gotta get to class.

IN DEFENSE OF "LOCAL ARTISTS"

I'm not sure how common this is in other scenes, but in hip hop, the phrase "local artist" is very often used pejoratively. It brings to mind that MC or producer who was never good enough to break out from their hometown, that starving artist playing the same sets at the same dive bars, year after year.

To be sure, that does happen. You're never going to be famous and sell lots of records if you focus all of your energy on just one community. But the assumption that every artist's goal is to "be famous and sell lots of records" is a dangerous one. The assumption that playing 200 shows in 200 cities has more inherent value than cultivating a substantive presence in your hometown is a dangerous one. And the assumption that anyone who talks about this stuff is just making excuses or "aiming low" isn't healthy for the culture or for our communities.

When I think about the artists who have had the biggest impact on me, the artists who have actually changed my life, very few of them are nationally-known. Or if they are nationally-known, it's just a side-effect of the work they do in their communities. Almost all of them could be classified as "local artists," even if the locales are different. They're people doing important, concrete work in their communities, using art not just to express themselves, but to carve out space within those communities for positive things to happen. They're using their art to create platforms for other kinds of media, for organizing, for education, for a whole host of goals that go far beyond fame and fortune.

Obviously, being engaged locally and being famous are not mutually exclusive. Someone like Boots Riley of the Coup can have an international following while still doing great work in Oakland. Invincible in Detroit, the Figureheads in Milwaukee, Geologic in

Seattle, Jasiri X in Pittsburgh—this list could go on and on. None of these artists may be household names, but the impact they've had and are having is undeniable.

Of course, the more famous you are, the more of a platform you have to spread whatever message you want to spread. I'm not arguing that being famous is bad. I'm just saying that I have a lot of respect for artists who consider fame as a means to an end, and not an end in and of itself. This isn't about scolding anyone for not being "conscious" enough; this is simply about recognizing the potential that artists (from the most revolutionary slam poet to the most apolitical shoegazing indie band or party rapper) have to be changemakers in our communities, in ways that go far beyond the occasional benefit concert.

This is about re-imagining the possibilities. I don't believe that the highest calling of an artist is to leave, to get famous and never look back. I don't even believe that art is the most important thing that artists have to offer.

I think about teaching artists, who go into schools and engage with young people around their art and identities. I think about artists who curate residencies at local venues. I think about artists who connect with activist organizations and use their social media following to signal boost messages that would otherwise not reach as many people. I think about all of the fundraisers, benefit shows, and rallies that are so much more exciting and community-oriented because of the presence of artists.

Art isn't just pretty pictures and catchy melodies. It's the lifeblood of a community. It's a platform to broadcast ideas. It's a tool to frame issues. It's a way to connect the past, present, and future. It's an excuse to bring living, breathing human beings together. I'm grateful to everyone who continues to do that. Keep building.

BEYOND THE BENEFIT: TEN WAYS ARTISTS CAN SUPPORT SOCIAL MOVEMENTS

I'm writing this in July of 2016, just a few months before the 2016 elections. It's stressful. At least part of that stress is knowing how important the next three months are going to be—not just because of the presidential election, but because of a whole host of other stuff on ballots around the country and here at home, plus the broader opportunity to *do* something with all of the energy, anger, and drive out here right now. A lot of us are trying to figure out how to best use whatever power, resources, or skills that we have to help make a difference.

So I'm thinking about the artist's role in helping to build a mass movement.

Of course, building a mass movement is everyone's job, and everyone has to figure out how best to leverage their strengths, passions, resources, access, etc. to contribute to the larger struggle. I think of teachers shifting their lesson plans in order to talk about current events. I think of religious leaders doing the same thing during their sermons. I think of workers organizing anti-oppression committees or even just book clubs in their workplaces. I think of athletes wearing #BlackLivesMatter shirts and refusing to be silent. I think of online communities, I think of students. I think of young people. Everyone has some kind of power or access to space that can help this movement grow.

When it comes to artists, this conversation usually begins and ends with our art. People talk about the power of narrative and framing, the power to make the abstract concrete, the power to touch people on an emotional level and transcend petty campaign politics. And I'm with that. But that's not the conversation that I want to have here. Because I believe that as artists, we have more to offer than our art.

I'm not asking artists to take leadership roles in social movements they may or may not know much about. I'm also not asking anyone to radically change their style or preferred subject matter, or be someone that they're not. I'm just saying that artists occupy strategically useful spaces in our communities, and have access to resources that can really help movements grow. In a perfect world, we'd all get directly involved in activist campaigns, but I know that reality doesn't always allow that to happen. So I'm trying to think of spaces of synergy. We can cheerlead stuff when it happens. But we can also use our platforms to help *make* stuff happen. What follows are ten ideas or potential starting points for how artists can make the most of that opportunity.

1. Commit and Get Connected

For me, this is first. This work has to be an intentional commitment, not just some random stuff we maybe do if someone *happens* to ask us to do it. Look at your calendar, from the top of August to the top of November. Are there particular opportunities that stand out? Really big shows? Tours? Interviews? All I'm saying here is have a plan, even if it's not 100% set-in-stone.

This also means getting connected. As artists, some of us have no idea what we're talking about, and that's okay. Some of us are super uncomfortable talking about things outside our comfort zone, and that's also okay. I want us all to educate ourselves, but more than that, I want us to connect to people who already know their stuff: organizers. Find the people in your community who are doing the work, and get in the loop—whether by following them on social media, reaching out via email, or showing up to actions.

2. To Get This Out of The Way: Yes, Raising Money Matters Too

The title of this piece is not saying that artists shouldn't play benefit shows; it's saying that we can do a lot *more* than that. That being said, raising money for organizations, campaigns, and projects can be a very powerful action. So, if this is something you are able to do, get in touch with activist organizations and make yourself available;

sometimes, that means playing a political fundraiser, and other times it means taking a space that isn't political and doing the work there anyway.

3. Intentional Signal-Boosting

I think that the baseline here is to find people who know what they're talking about, follow them on social media and/or in real life, and help boost their voices. Beyond that, though, the key word is intentionality. Retweeting people who know what they're talking about is good. Posting links to articles we think people should read is good. But I think a lot of this is done haphazardly—we happen to see something, and then happen to RT it. But a little extra thought can go a long way. A few tactics:

- Make more of an effort to signal-boost on-the-ground activists and not just media talking-heads. The latter group can have some great analysis, but boosting the voices of the people in the trenches is important. This also relates to making sure that we're signal-boosting the people who are directly affected by the issue (for example, Matt McGorry might have something good to say about intersectionality, but so do a lot of Black women, who have *been* saying good things).

- Whenever an artist with a lot of followers speaks out about an issue, that's good. But I also think that there is a continuum of value at play. Posting a statement or a rant is good. Posting a rant with a link to an article with more information is maybe better. Posting a rant with a link to an article *and* info on an upcoming action is better still.

- There are weeks when I don't post anything self-promotional. Just links and resources. And yeah, I lose some followers who aren't trying to hear that stuff, but I gain more. This isn't just altruism. Especially with how Facebook's algorithm works today (explicitly self-promotional posts are more likely to stay invisible to fans); posting about current events and struggles just makes sense.

4. Using Artist Space as Activist Space

The average club show is 4-5 hours long. If you have 3-4 acts on the bill, there is still plenty of time to be creative with how that space is used. The most obvious thing is to **share the mic:** invite local activists to speak between sets and promote what they're doing. Set them up with a table next to the merch table. This should be a regular, expected occurrence at shows.

We can also be more creative. I mean, you can do a lot with an hour of stage time. Most of us just perform for an hour, maybe with some awkward banter between songs/poems. But what else can we do? Some of the most rewarding experiences I've had on stage have been when I've decided to *not* just do my ten best songs or whatever, and really try to connect to the audience, to have a conversation, to do something together beyond "look at me for an hour because I'm great."

At one show, we took a big chalkboard and I asked audience members to write down actions they could take regarding police brutality and the prison-industrial complex. This was during those twenty minutes at every show between the listed start-time and the actual start-time. By the time we did start the show, the board was full of ideas. I'm not saying that that's the most transformative thing you can do on stage, but I think it is an example of how breaking the fourth wall and being more interactive can really add to the power of an event. Have a discussion. Play a short video. Stage theatrical disruptions. Be creative. We frown upon teachers who just lecture for an hour straight; I think we can hold performing artists to a similar standard.

We can also re-think the idea of the merch table. Yes, you have your CDs, vinyl, and shirts. But it's such a simple thing to also include handouts, literature, petitions, or whatever else from local organizers. Again, this is not any kind of radical reconceptualization of how we do our work. This is easy, but stuff like this can make a difference—especially in the context of the next point.

5. A Tour Is Never Just a Tour

Let's think critically about the power that we have as touring artists. To use my community as an example: we know that in elections, cities (especially the Twin Cities) generally vote progressive, and the suburbs and rural areas generally don't. Obviously, a lot of this has to with demographics, but there's also the fact that progressive campaigns are easier to organize in big cities. So who has access to thousands of people outside of the metro area? Touring artists. When we play shows in Bemidji or Brainerd or Winona or Duluth or Rochester or St. Cloud or Morris or wherever (including the Twin Cities, because we shouldn't make the assumption that everyone here is "already down," since they're not), that's a tremendous opportunity. We can connect to activists in those cities too, and figure out how we might help boost their efforts. Touring artists have the potential to reach and influence thousands of potential voters and potential activists– especially if the previous two points are involved.

6. Shoot a PSA

If you're even a halfway-successful artist, people are paying attention to you. People like some aspect of what you're about. Maybe they just think you're cute. Maybe they think you're brilliant. Maybe they just like you because their friends like you—it doesn't matter. You can take advantage of your position by shooting a simple PSA, even just on your phone or laptop. It can be short and informal, or super well thought out like a speech or TEDx Talk or whatever. Where social media posts are somewhat transitory, a video might have longer "legs" in terms of getting seen by more and more people.

7. Remember that Networks Aren't Just About Social Media

When we talk about signal-boosting and network-sharing, it's easy to focus on social media. But as artists, our networks run deeper than our likes and followers. We can mobilize people. When we've made connections to organizations, maybe played a fundraiser or two, done some signal-boosting, etc., these partnerships can evolve into something deeper and stronger. This will look different in different contexts; maybe the point here is that we have to be open to ideas, strategies, and actions that don't fit neatly into a ten-point bullet point list.

Projects, initiatives, and campaigns pop up all the time, and being plugged in already is vital to being able to truly support them in ways that transcend signal-boosting. I know this point is a little more abstract than the others, but we're talking about what it means to really be part of a community, as opposed to just applauding that community.

8. Don't Be Afraid to Be Timely Instead of Timeless

All of the points on this list can be acted upon even if you're not a super political artist. From navel-gazing indie bands to party rappers to club DJs—everyone can do this work. Sometimes the most effective "political" events aren't actually explicitly political; if you can get people to come to a show who don't care about the issues, and then make those issues part of that show, you're reaching a valuable audience.

Art is beautiful and important, but I really believe that it's the relationships around the art, the community built by art, and the networks cultivated by art that matter even more. That being said, we are artists, and one thing that we can always do is make art about the issues that we care about. Especially if you're one of those aforementioned artists who isn't known for being political—that just means you can make a bigger splash when you *do* release a song that grapples with an issue.

It would be beyond the scope of this piece to really dig into what makes political art more effective vs. less effective. Use your style, your voice, your perspective. Don't try to speak for other people; tackle issues from your own position. Think about who your audience is and how you might reach them. Collaborate. Experiment. Have fun.

9. Lead by Example

This is a point that transcends election season, but how can we use our position(s) in the community to fight for lasting political and cultural change? What might it mean if artists refuse to play venues that have bad reputations in terms of their staff/security's relationship with patrons of color? Or refuse to play venues that don't offer gender-neutral restrooms? Or refuse to jump on a bill or sit on a panel when everyone is white? Or male? What might it mean to hold your local media, venues, radio, etc. accountable? This will look different in different scenes, of course. It can also be proactive instead of reactive: what might it look like to collaborate across genres and scenes on a community-oriented project? What might it look like to invest in alternative media or other local systems/structures? How can we do more to pass on skills and opportunities to the next generation? The possibilities are endless.

10. Dive In and Get Involved

This won't be an option for everyone, but the best way to make a difference is still to just show up and get engaged. Join an organization. Go to meetings. As artists, we have a lot of useful skills (press/media relations, flyer design, web/social media management, systems thinking, speechwriting, event organizing, and much more) that might only get a chance to be fully activated if we're down there in the streets with the activists and organizers who really fuel this movement. Make banners. Write chants. Write press releases.

Activism is about relationships. Even if you can't formally sign on and attend weekly meetings, those relationships are vital. That kind of brings us full-circle back to point #1. Connect. If nothing else, connect. Again, the key word in all of this is "intentional." A lot of artists are on some "I don't want to be preachy; my music encourages people to think for themselves." But right now, in the world we live in? That feels like a cop-out. It feels like wasted potential. It feels like, to paraphrase Howard Zinn, trying to stand still on a moving train.

Sharing resources isn't being preachy. Connecting your art to movement-building efforts doesn't make you self-important. It's just a concrete, effective way to leverage the fact that we have audiences, audiences that activist movements can't always reach as easily. That's power—and it means nothing if it isn't acted upon.

As artists, we talk a lot about planting seeds. But there is a difference between scattering wildflower seeds haphazardly as we skip through the meadow, and planting crops with intention and care. Wildflowers can be beautiful, but crops are revolutionary. Crops can feed your family. "Doing good work" is easy. "Building a movement" takes *more* than that. Thankfully, I know that my community is up to that challenge.

WHY AREN'T THERE MORE FEMALE MCS? A CASE STUDY IN HOW SEXISM WORKS

A few years ago, I wrote a piece on sexism in indie hip hop, and it's something that continues to get traffic to this day, possibly because there aren't a ton of people talking about the issue. One part of that piece that I think deserves a closer look is representation. At every level of the game—from platinum-selling superstars to hungry indie rappers to basement hobbyists—men outnumber women and gender-nonconforming artists by sizable, indisputable margins.

Of course, there are many great MCs who aren't men—Psalm One, Jean Grae, Nicki Minaj, Lauryn Hill and more, plus locals like Maria Isa, Desdamona, Irenic, The Lioness, Lizzo, Dessa, BdotCroc and others. But proportionately, *there should be many more*. And the explanations we so often hear: "hip hop is about aggression and women can't do that as well," or "girls would rather sing than rap," are just too shallow.

By taking a deeper look at why women are underrepresented in hip hop, I think we can shed some light on why this is true in other areas of society as well. Sexism, after all, is bigger than just face-to-face misogyny or discrimination; it's embedded into our culture in sometimes invisible, insidious ways.

One note: this is not about hip hop's special relationship with sexism. I'm using hip hop as a lens here because I'm most familiar with it, but I'm sure the same stuff plays out in indie rock, novel writing, competitive axe throwing, stand-up comedy, the U.S. Senate and many other cultures. I just think the lack of women's representation among hip hop artists is a great entry point to exploring how sexism functions in other realms.

Level 1: Cultivating a Love for the Music

It starts with the music. You hear a song, you like it. It has a nice beat, maybe a cool video. One song leads to another, leads to an album, a discography, affiliated artists, a deluge of music. For me, it was Goodie Mob, into Outkast, into Tribe, into Wu-Tang and beyond. For a kid today, it might be Kendrick Lamar, or Odd Future, or Macklemore, or someone else. There's the gateway, and then there's the path.

But look at all those artists I just mentioned. They're all men. Some of them are explicitly misogynistic men. So even at this very first level of progression, young women face a hurdle—even if they like the music on a sonic level, there are far fewer women to relate to and see as role models. Add to this the fact that a significant portion of the men on the radio are saying terrible things about women, and we're not off to a great start.

Level 2: Exploring the Art Form

Still, many young women will persevere and develop a love for not just listening to rap, but creating it too. This process can take many forms—maybe you just start freestyling with your friends at the lunch table, or participate in a hip hop youth arts program, or you have a relative who shows you around their home studio.

But again, sexism impacts the journey. Because of the various level 1 hurdles, it's more likely that your lunch-table friends who rap will be guys. Will they accept you? Will you feel comfortable in that space? We have an image of the fiery young woman who knocks down the door into the boy's club and gains acceptance through sheer pluck and determination; but what if you're not an instant virtuoso? Or an extrovert? Will the men who facilitate the hip hop arts programs push you into singing the hook or writing a poem instead of rapping? Will all the airtime be taken up by the boys? Who owns the studio? Who mixes the tracks? Who's making the beats? Who can be a mentor? I know this is anecdotal, but I don't think anyone will argue the fact: it's men, men, men.

I'm not saying that women can't relate to or network with guys. But part of male privilege is the ease with which we form these relationships. Sexism may not always be about an explicit, discriminatory act; sometimes it's just about the lack of this kind of privilege, the additional hurdle, the uphill battle.

Level 3: Building Your Career

But again, some will persevere. Let's say a young woman is now very much an MC, with a style, some experience, and an album's worth of songs to give to the world. What's next?

The answer is a lot more networking. Making music is one thing; getting it heard is something else entirely. Now you need to reach out not just to fans, but to the tastemakers and gatekeepers who can get you to your potential fans: college radio DJs, hip hop bloggers, local music writers, booking agents, promoters and other artists. I probably don't have to say it at this point, but statistically, these are almost all going to be guys.

It's important to note that some of them may be nice, supportive guys, too. But it's still about the ease of the relationship, the ability to relate to another person's story, the subconscious ways we judge each other based on appearance and identity. And sure, some of them *will* be creeps, which doesn't help.

Level 4: Getting Famous, or Just Making a Living

If you want to be successful as an MC, it comes down to some combination of talent, work ethic, networks, and pure capture-the-zeitgeist marketability/luck. And each one of these factors is impacted by the communities through which we move.

Your talent is your own, but the quality of your music will always be impacted by your collaborators—which producers you can get to work with you, what kind of mentoring relationships you can set up, who you can call on for guest spots, etc. You may be the hardest worker in your city, but hustle doesn't happen in a vacuum; you're constantly building with people, attempting to persuade a particular audience to give you a shot, contacting DJs, promoters and more. *All* of this is impacted by male privilege and sexism, as we've seen at each level so far.

There's more: will music writers talk about your music, or will they just talk about how you're a "femcee?" Will potential fans give you a shot even if you're not conventionally pretty, since our society places so much value on women's appearances? Can you rap about whatever you want, or will you be expected to speak for all women everywhere? If you want to have a family, will your partner take care of the kids while you're on tour, or will you be expected to do that? The list goes on.

This is what we mean when we talk about male privilege. It's not that men "have it easy;" being successful is hard no matter who you are. It's just that women (or more accurately: anyone who doesn't identify as a stereotypically masculine man) face these additional hurdles, and they're hurdles that, as men, we sometimes don't even have to think about.

It's Bigger than Hip Hop

I can't stress this enough: this isn't just about rap. This is how sexism works everywhere. It's not always about the word "bitch" or the boss sexually harassing his assistant. It's about the male-dominated networks that have been built over the course of decades. It's about the "good ol' boys" club and how advancement in any system is tied to your ability to relate to the men at the top. It's about seeing a 95-to-5 male-to-female imbalance in a particular institution and thinking that that's perfectly normal.

The good news is that there's plenty we can do about all this. With hip hop, solutions may lie in more intentional concert lineups, programs set up specifically to reach out to young women who want to rap (or produce, or DJ, etc.), artists of all gender identities speaking out on this issue, and all of us as listeners actively promoting the artists we support through our tweets, our Facebook walls, and especially our dollars.

In other cultures and communities, solutions may look different. But whether it's through building alternative institutions or organizing for change within existing ones, we can make a difference. The first step is forcing ourselves to see the full scope of the problem. The second step is understanding that, no matter what communities we navigate through, we have the power to do something about it.

MEN'S RIGHTS ACTIVISTS AND THE NEW SEXISM

As an artist who talks a lot about gender issues, I've run across men's rights activists (MRAs) here and there over the past few years, never giving them much thought. But last week, a video of poet Kait Rokowski's darkly satirical poem "How to Cure a Feminist" that I host on my YouTube channel went viral, and suddenly my inbox was inundated with comment notifications. I read all of them. A few examples:

"Sorry I'm pro equality, but feminism is a Rockefeller funded cult that hijacked the women's rights movement. Trying to fight against peoples [sic] way of life is wrong."

"Well it really depends what you mean by 'feminism'. If you mean equality of rights for sexes then that's great and that already happened in the west. If you mean dismantling patriarchy and rape culture and so on then it quickly verges on bunk."

"Chauvinism is an ugly part of the human condition regardless of the perpetrators [sic] gender."

"In some sense I find this poem to be sexist against men as it suggests most men express negative feelings towards all women."

I realize that YouTube comments are the lowest form of human communication, but these are still fascinating. This is what sexism looks like in 2013: it's not "Women sure are worthless and stupid" as much as it is "I'm a good guy who loves and respects women but feminism is evil because the systematic oppression of women doesn't really exist."

It's a more "well-intentioned" sexism, and it's just as harmful. I'm sure there are all kinds of internal ideological struggles in the MRA movement (just like there are in feminism), but this is a consistent undercurrent. They believe in a kind of equality, but also that women's movements have overreached—making men the new victims of sexism.

Women have made great strides in recent decades, after all, closing many gaps in higher ed graduation rates, improving media representation and earning more and more money. But has it been enough to compensate for centuries of inequality? Have these strides benefited all women equally? Have they benefitted gender-nonconforming people and trans women? Have these strides translated into power? How many women presidents have we had? Congresspeople? Governors? Generals and admirals? CEOs and billionaires? Which gender is still stereotyped as strong, assertive, responsible and tough, and which is still stereotyped as passive, nurturing, dependent, and overly emotional? I don't need to quote statistics here—sexism saturates our culture; it's everywhere.

My female boss is mean to me at work is not the same thing as centuries of institutionalized, systemic discrimination. If *beautiful women can get whatever they want*, then why haven't we elected one president yet? *Sexism against both genders is wrong* betrays a fundamental misunderstanding of what sexism is. Any individual of any gender can be prejudiced or discriminate on a face-to-face level, but who faces the glass ceiling, the ongoing, legalized regulation of their bodies, the significant wage gap for doing the same type of work, the deeply-ingrained cultural assumptions and ill-informed stereotypes about their being less aggressive, less capable and less intelligent, and countless other obstacles?

And the thing is, men *are* hurt by sexism. Rigid gender roles, for example, aren't healthy for anyone. But it is not the same kind of hurt, and feminism definitely isn't the enemy—it's an invaluable analysis, a frame through which we can start to work toward real liberation for people of all gender identities.

The first step, however, is acknowledging that sexism—as in the historical and institutional economic, cultural, and psychological oppression of women (and gender nonconforming people)—is real. If we can't start there, then we are working with band-aids, individual solutions to complex, large-scale social problems.

The lesson here is not that we should all go pick fights with MRAs; they're an easy target. It's that we should challenge ourselves to understand sexism (and racism, and homophobia, etc.) in this larger sense—it's not just individual acts of harassment or discrimination, and the solution to it has to be bigger than "being better" on an individual level.

WHY I'M THANKFUL FOR FEMINISM

Because this is a follow-up to last week's column on Men's Rights Activists, it's tempting to frame it as "an open letter to MRAs and critics of feminism." But I'm not going to do that, for two reasons:

1. Let's be honest: arguing in circles about terminology and engaging in endless link wars over studies and statistics never really convinces anyone of anything.

2. In the social justice movement, we spend far too much time distracted by extreme minorities of people who are never going to agree with us anyway. If 10,000 people read this, the percentage who identify as MRAs will be a drop in the bucket compared to social media friends, internet surfers, students doing research, etc. So I'd rather write something for them.

Even though some commenter last week bizarrely demanded that I tell "the truth" instead of just "my truth," I can't really do that. I can only share my own experiences with feminism and feminists.

I got my start as an activist around the 2003 Iraq war protests. I was young and had no idea what I was doing, but I was constantly supported by all kinds of people—socialists, anarchists, artists, union organizers, students, hippies, veterans, moderates, and people from all identities and walks of life. The self-identified feminists, in particular, were some of the most effective activists I encountered.

Because of ongoing debates within feminism, they had a firm grasp on the importance of intersectionality (a term coined by scholar Kimberlé Crenshaw)—understanding how struggles are linked, and highlighting the connections between different oppressions. They were also just good activists—able to write press releases, canvas door-to-door, speak in front of crowds, facilitate meetings and all the little things that go into any movement.

I wish I didn't have to point this out, but I do: none of them hated men. None of them advocated for female supremacy. Most of them were women of color. Most of them were working class. A few of them identified as gender-nonconforming. None of them fit the stereotype. It makes one wonder where that stereotype comes from, and why it persists.

Today, my job takes me all over the country, performing and facilitating workshops on social justice concepts. Since many of the organizations that book me work on gender issues, I get to meet and talk with feminists with countless different philosophies and approaches to the work.

Some of the stuff they're working on: challenging rape culture, cultivating critical thinking skills and media literacy, working in solidarity with other organizations and their causes, advocating for healthy sexuality and access to effective sexual education, raising awareness around sexual assault in the military, fighting for trans rights, organizing for the inclusion of gender-neutral restrooms in public buildings, providing resources for people going through intimate partner violence, holding leaders and media personalities accountable for their words and actions, defending a woman's right to choose, challenging the rigidity of gender roles, organizing discussion groups for men around healthy masculinity, engaging in educational work around body image, and a million other things.

Again, notice that there's nothing here about elevating women over men, or making men feel bad, or using blood magic to turn your daughters into witches. Most of these campaigns help men too. Most of these struggles are reactions to (often urgent) existing problems. All over the country, feminists are fighting for gender equity, because that fight continues to be necessary.

I'm trying to get at two things by sharing all this. For the MRAs, I just want to say: I know a lot more real-life feminists (as opposed to strawradfem strangers on Tumblr) than you do, and they're committed, effective organizers who don't fit your stereotypes at all. And for the rest of us, I want to say: one of the reasons that feminism is important is that it provides a framework not just for theory and ideology, but for action.

I could quote bell hooks over and over again, but this is a good one: "Simply put, feminism is a movement to end sexism, sexist exploitation and oppression." She wrote this in "Feminist Theory: From the Margin to the Center," and revisited it more recently in the excellent "Feminism is for Everybody: Passionate Politics." I like this definition because it's pretty straightforward, and also frames feminism not just as a theory, but as a movement.

It's one thing to say "I'm one of the good guys" or "let's all just be egalitarians," but does that change anything? If you want to fight sexism, whether you're a feminist, an MRA, or anyone, you have to actively fight sexism. It is not enough to just "be cool and hope for the best." And feminism provides a rich history of action, approaches to activism, toolkits, and much more.

I'm thankful for feminism because feminists work on issues that affect me and the people I love. I'm thankful for feminism because it proves that movements can evolve, from a movement of "rich white ladies" to a movement that understands how identities are intertwined and how liberation must be an ongoing, simultaneous process. More than anything, though, I'm thankful for feminism because it proves that people working together can actually make a difference. If we fight for the things we care about, we can win.

Feminism isn't the only movement that demonstrates that, of course. And there are plenty of super legitimate criticisms of specific campaigns, individual activists and thought-currents within the larger movement. But if we are ever able to forge a coalition that can challenge injustice and oppression at every level, a feminist analysis is going to be part of it, and I'm thankful for that.

A Series of Essays on Race

AN OPEN LETTER TO WHITE PEOPLE ABOUT TRAYVON MARTIN

This was originally published the night after the Zimmerman verdict, where it maxed out the comment system of the blog that hosted it. I'm including it in this book because I think it's still relevant, sadly.

In the next few days, there are going to be a lot of essays and op-eds attempting to make sense of, or grapple with, or process the Zimmerman verdict, from writers who are better than me. So I want to talk about this from a very specific angle.

This is an open letter to white people, especially to those white people who understand that something terrible has happened, and has been happening, and will continue to happen, but don't know what to do.

Clearly, something needs to change. But not every problem has a clear-cut, run-out-the-door-and-do-something solution. If you're angry, or sad, take a second to process. Think about where you fit into this injustice, how you benefit from it, how you're hurt by it. If that involves prayers, or posting links on Twitter, or having hard conversations, or writing poems, do that. Process.

But it can't end with "processing."

If you're someone who has avoided thinking about white privilege—the unearned advantages that white people benefit from because of how institutions are set up and how history has unfolded—now is a great time to unstick your head from the sand. If Trayvon Martin had been white, he'd still be alive. What better real-world example of white privilege is there? Grappling with how privilege plays out in our own lives is a vital first step to being able to understand what racism is.

But it can't end with "thinking about our privilege."

We also need to act on those thoughts, to cultivate an awareness that can permeate our lives and relationships. When people of color share personal stories about racism, our immediate response has to stop being "but I'm not like that." Just listen. Don't make someone else's oppression about you and your feelings. When people of color are angry, we need to stop worrying about the tone of their arguments, or trying to derail the conversation with phrases like "it's not just about race," or contribute meaningless abstractions like "yeah, let's start a revolution." When we see unjust or discriminatory practices or attitudes in our workplaces, schools, families or neighborhoods, we need to step up and challenge them. We need to take risks. We need to do better.

But it can't end with "striving to be a better individual."

Times like this can feel so hopeless, but it's important to remember that people are fighting back, and have been fighting back. Racism doesn't end when you decide to not be racist. It ends when people come together to organize, to work to reshape how our society is put together.

Check out organizations that are doing racial justice work, community organizing trainings, work with youth, and more. Google stuff. Talk to people (especially other white people; don't rely on people of color to be your personal tutors). Figure out where and how you can plug in. As a white person, that can be hard. The leaders of any racial justice movement will be, and should be, the people who are most affected by the problem. But that doesn't mean that white people should just sit by and watch. Some organizations may have ways for you to get involved; some might not. But there's always something you can do. Organize a discussion group. Learn about good ally behavior. Challenge your Facebook friends. Challenge yourself. Join an organization. Infuse social justice principles into your workplace, or place of worship, or school, or neighborhood. Go into a career that might put you in a position to help create institutional change. Listen. Understand that Trayvon Martin's murder was not an isolated incident; start seeing the racism all around you, and start doing something about it.

Above all, stay engaged. As white people, we have the option of not caring. Many don't.

HOW TO COMPLETELY MISS THE POINT IN A CONVERSATION ABOUT RACISM

This was originally published a week after the previous essay was published.

"Telling [people of color] they're obsessed with racism is like telling a drowning person they're obsessed with swimming."
—Hari Kondabolu

After a week of comments and conversations, I wanted to address the recurring points that some white people have brought up in the wake of the Zimmerman verdict. Because it's not just about Trayvon Martin; every time there's a national conversation about race and racism, white people (yes, I'm generalizing; no, I'm not sorry) tend to have the same kinds of reactions.

Getting wildly, irrationally defensive even though it's not about you

My column from last week basically just says "if you're white and upset about the verdict, here are some things you can do to confront racism in your own life." That's it.

But then come the comments: "It's racist to say that white people are racist!" "Why do we have to make such a big deal out of this?" "I'm white and I went to go to college so there's no such thing as white privilege!" "Why do we have to be singled out?" "The people talking about racism are the real racists!" "We're not all like that!" "I'm so offended!"

White people: "talking about racism" does not equal "attacking you personally." We desperately need to stop being so insecure every time anyone brings up anything remotely related to race and racism. You don't have to agree, but to immediately jump into "eyes-closed-and-screaming" mode speaks volumes about you and the kind of world in which you'd prefer to live.

Refusing to acknowledge the role that race plays in our lives

"It wasn't about race." That was the most consistent theme in the responses. Time and time again, when there is a racial incident in this country, people of color point to the giant racist elephant rampaging through the room and white people say "oh that's probably just the wind."

Is it possible that Zimmerman would have approached a white kid the same way he approached Trayvon Martin? Sure... it's *possible*. But the lived experience of millions upon millions of people says that it's also extremely naïve to believe that that would actually happen.

When people of color talk about racism, they're not just making things up. There's no Black Santa who delivers big bags of money to anyone who claims to have been discriminated against. Racial profiling, harassment and discrimination are daily realities for millions of people. To just dismiss that as "whining" or "playing the race card" is unbelievably arrogant.

"Refusing to talk about racism" doesn't end racism. "Ending racism" ends racism. If your house is on fire, you don't just ignore the flames away. Maybe a better metaphor is if your neighbors' house is on fire, you don't tell them to "stop making such a big deal out of it." You don't look the other direction and say "but are you sure it's on fire?" You help, or you get the hell out of the way.

Focusing on the details and ignoring the big picture

"Zimmerman was half-Peruvian!" "911 dispatchers don't have the authority to give orders!" "Trayvon was big and really strong and got in trouble at school!" "Zimmerman had an African- American girlfriend once!" "Since Trayvon was right-handed, and standing at x angle, and the moon was at y point in the sky, there's no way he could have..."

Stop.

I think the biggest misconception about the outrage around the Zimmerman trial is that people are mad about the verdict. To be fair, many are. But many more are mad because Travyon Martin happens every day in this country. It may not always end with a dramatic gun death, but young Black and brown men are demonized, profiled, harassed, imprisoned and killed every day for being young Black and brown men (and women too, let's be honest).

The marches and rallies that have been happening recently aren't just about Trayvon Martin. They're about the culture that demonizes Black and brown youth, assuming that they're dangerous, threatening, and up-to-no-good. They're about the lack of accountability and consequences in police brutality cases. They're about disproportionate minority confinement. They're about the selective application of the "Stand Your Ground" law. They're about the gross over-representation of people of color in the criminal justice system. They're about who is given the benefit of the doubt and who isn't, time and time again. They're about the continued de-valuing of Black and brown life in this country.

Argue about the specific details of this specific case all you want, but nothing in the above paragraph is up for debate. That's the big picture that we—especially those of us who identify as white—have to see, if we ever hope to transition from "having a conversation about racism" to "doing something about racism."

PRACTICAL WAYS WE CAN STOP CENTERING EVERYTHING AROUND WHITE PEOPLE'S FEELINGS

Originally published about six months after the previous two pieces.

Fun fact: white people's feelings are magic. They can bring any conversation, meeting, or movement to a halt. In a debate, they can outweigh even the most credible, concrete evidence. They can threaten someone's job. They can even kill. White people's feelings are one of this country's most abundant natural resources and important exports.

Because of all this, any conversation about social justice, power, or history is going to naturally settle into orbit around white people's feelings. And I get it: if we want to really do something about racism in this country, it's white people who need to change the most, and it's white people who often have the longest political/spiritual/emotional journey to undertake.

But when social justice education and/or media focuses solely on understanding racism through a white privilege framework, that can recreate the same oppressive structures we're trying to destroy. When the conversation has such a laser focus around educating white people and carrying their emotional baggage, what potential voices, perspectives, or frameworks are missing? We may be moving forward, but how are we defining "we?"

As someone who is both a social justice educator and who identifies as at least somewhat white myself, I'd like to explore some other options. How else can we engage in anti-racist work without having everything be about white people's feelings? A few possibilities:

Separate Spaces

This kind of work is already happening, but I think it's worth noting: we can continue to develop programming that is specifically for white people (alongside programming that is specifically for any identity group) rather than relying on the "catch-all" approach that alienates, bores, or infuriates so many students (specifically students of color). In these spaces, we can talk about white people's feelings without having that conversation derail the other important work that's happening. "Caucusing" can be controversial, but it can also be effective.

Triage

Maybe that's a strong word, but in social justice education spaces, we can acknowledge that some material is going to make white people (or men, or straight people, or any other privileged group) sad. Or angry. Or guilty, confused, defensive, etc. And we can acknowledge that, and then we can just keep moving. As a facilitator, it's not your job to "save" anyone. As an educator, you want to get your point across and cultivate understanding, but when all of the energy in the room goes into making a handful of defensive white students feel better, that's not healthy or productive for the larger group.

Sometimes, Education Isn't the Answer

Sometimes, the personal/cultural change happens after the institution has already moved on. There may be times when the funding, time, and energy poured into "diversity education" initiatives could perhaps be better spent changing the fundamental structure of the institution. We can teach an all-white board of directors about the importance of racially-inclusive language, for example, or we can fight to get people of color on the board of directors. Education is always going to be part of the larger movement toward racial justice, but that doesn't mean that it is the absolute answer in every scenario. Clearly, education and organizing are not mutually exclusive (just the opposite), but as the saying goes, "the work is not the workshop."

White People: Do Your Homework

Most of the points on this list are for educators and organizers who work in these spaces. But those of us who are white can do more, proactively, even outside these spaces. Read books. Listen. Suppress the urge to always get defensive about everything. Never rely on someone else to do the emotional dirty work for you, or hold your hand.

Brave Spaces vs. Safe Spaces

I'm not sure who came up with this framework, but I think it's useful. In any social justice education space, it's worth acknowledging that it's *good* to be challenged and to be uncomfortable, especially if we're carrying privilege with us into that space. Of course, we need to take care of ourselves, but "taking care of yourself" should never mean "sticking your head in the sand to avoid all criticism and/or difficult conversations."

A common thread in all of these points is that change isn't predicated on anyone's feelings; change is the product of collaborative, intentional work. Education matters—and even white people's feelings matter— but only as much as they make that work easier or harder.

When all of the energy in a particular educational campaign or organization is poured into making sure the people who already carry the most privilege aren't getting their feelings hurt, that hurts movements. We can do better.

Nothing I'm saying here is new; these are ongoing conversations that will continue to shift, evolve, and come to new conclusions. I also, clearly, have my own baggage and biases around this topic. But I hope this can help lead to more thought, more discussion, and more action.

A VISIT FROM THE PC POLICE

Okay, class, settle down. No, you can't touch my gun. No, none of you are going to get tased today. See, I'm not a regular cop, so my presentation this afternoon is not going to be about drugs or graffiti. I'm with a special unit... the division of political correctness—yes, the PC police.

And I know that we don't have a good reputation, that everyone thinks we're just trying to stamp out free speech, or create a world where everyone lies to themselves, and it's all sunshine, lollipops, and unicorns. I get that. No one likes being told what to do. But the thing is, political correctness isn't about being perfect, or censoring your emotions or always being nice to everyone. It's just about *not* being a jackass.

For example, the word "retarded" is offensive to a lot of people because it dehumanizes those with cognitive or developmental disabilities. So when you use that word to talk about the plot of the new action movie blockbuster, or make fun of your friend for forgetting his wallet, you're kind of being a jackass.

Similarly, rape is a real thing that happens to real people, far too often, ~~no one should joke about it only be used when actually talking about rape~~ not in ironically over-the-top comedy routines, not when referring to what a bad 3D conversion did to your eyes, and not when talking about how that video game mini-boss took down your shields in one shot. With all of these examples, it's not that your feelings are wrong, it's just that you're expressing those feelings like a jackass.

Fun fact: the word "bitch" is a derogatory term for woman. And unless you are a principled third-wave feminist attempting to reclaim the word, which you're probably not, it does not matter how you're using it—as an all-purpose, ungendered insult, as a synonym for "complain," or as a directionless expletive at the end of a particularly vicious rap verse—it is *always* a derogatory term for woman. You cannot give a chicken-salad sandwich to a vegetarian and say "but it's chicken *salad*."

Am I saying that you are a bad person if you use these words? No. Am I saying that I've never used these words? No. Am I saying that it should be *illegal* for anyone to use these words? Absolutely not.

I'm just saying this: most people use offensive language because they just don't know any better. But there are others out there who like to be offensive, because they think it's cool. Here's the thing about that: you want to be edgy, you want to push people's buttons? Talk about white privilege. Talk about drone strikes, police brutality, or the foreclosure crisis. Talk about rape culture. Those things will push people out of their comfort zones, more than "using naughty words" ever could.

You want to go against the grain and be that cool, independent rebel? Good. Do that. I'm just saying there are more powerful ways to do that than needlessly shitting on entire communities of people who already have an uphill battle in this society. Using inclusive language is very easy. If you think it's hard, that's because you're not really trying.

Now, if I were to say "don't ever use the letter W because that letter is offensive to me," then you could get mad. It would be very difficult to go through life without using the letter W. That would be an unreasonable request.

But do white people ever *need* to use the n-word? Is it so difficult to say that you got "screwed" instead of you got "jewed?" Can you think of no better way to register your dislike for something than to call it "gay?"

Shakespeare once wrote: "A most notable coward, an infinite and endless liar, an hourly promise breaker, the owner of no one good quality. Thy tongue outvenoms all the worms of Nile. Thine face is not worth sunburning." Now, that's not all from one passage, but still, what a glorious, beautiful way to call someone a jackass.

You may have noticed that I've used the word "jackass" numerous times during this presentation. That's because even though "jackass" is an insult, it's the *good* kind of insult. It's a word that disrespects people who are rude, annoying, and thoughtless by comparing them to donkeys. And sure, it may be offensive to donkeys—but who gives a shit?

Class, I'm two weeks away from retirement. I've been fighting the good fight since teenagers were calling each other "gay-wads" and politicians were openly using racial slurs in campaign speeches.

And I know, you may not have anything against people with disabilities, or women, or the LGBTQ community or anyone, but using language like this—even if you don't *mean* it to be offensive, directly contributes to a culture that hurts people.

And sure, we need to do a lot more than just change the way we talk, but... I'm just a beat cop. I hope you'll all be my deputies. Together, we can say "no" to being a jackass.

EIGHT INVALID ARGUMENTS REGARDING POP CULTURE AND OFFENSIVENESS

Part of being passionate about art and culture is getting into arguments about art and culture. I've had my share, especially when it comes to the intersection of social justice and pop culture. What follows are eight rhetorical devices I've encountered in these arguments and why I don't buy them.

1. "It's just a (movie/song/book/commercial/etc.)"

Culture informs society. To dismiss pop culture as pure escapism or background noise is naïve. No, hearing Eminem say *stab you in the head/ whether you're a fag or lez* isn't going to instantly turn every listener into a violent homophobe, but to say that there isn't any impact at all is just intellectually dishonest.

Offensive images and words, over time, do help shape the world, especially when those images or words correspond with institutions that systematically oppress people. Even seemingly innocuous archetypes like "the sassy Black friend" or the "wise old Asian man" in movies become harmful because of the prevalence of the images and the lack of alternative images.

2. "You're just being over-sensitive. Lighten up."

When someone is offended, that emotional and intellectual response is real. It's arrogant to simply write that off. Maybe the person really is misinterpreting something, but the least you can do is take a second to try to understand where they're coming from and consider the specific points they're making. If someone thinks that James Cameron's "Avatar" co-opts and distorts indigenous struggles, and you disagree, talk about why you disagree; don't just dismiss them as a whiny baby. Better yet, suppress the impulse to immediately debate them and just listen.

It's also worth noting that finding something offensive isn't always about "hurt feelings." It's often also about recognizing the connections between offensive words or images and dangerous, oppressive systems and institutions. The "this isn't a big deal" attitude reveals a fundamental naïveté about how culture informs society; see point #1.

3. "My friend is (Asian/lesbian/blind/etc.) and she wasn't offended."

Your friend is not the absolute authority on all things (Asian/lesbian/blind/etc.). If other people are offended, that reaction is real; see point #2. Asian-American actors from "Miss Saigon" have defended the play; their support, however, doesn't make other people's critiques invalid.

4. "At least it's better than everything else out there."

Eating light bulbs is better for you than drinking bleach; that doesn't mean eating light bulbs is a good thing. The current state of pop culture is pretty awful when it comes to representation and social justice. Being "a little bit better" isn't good enough to exempt anyone from criticism. It's great that Joss Whedon writes strong female characters; we can still criticize him, however, for his treatment of characters of color.

5. "Sure it was offensive, but they didn't mean it to be. They weren't trying to be (racist, sexist, homophobic, etc). They just didn't know better."

If you accidentally offend someone, you might not be a bad person, but it does not magically absolve you of responsibility. Impact trumps intent. Saying something hurtful out of ignorance is only marginally better than saying something hurtful out of malice, and the effect on people is exactly the same. Katy Perry may not have anything against the LGBTQ community, but the song "Ur So Gay" still reinforces hurtful stereotypes. Fans of the Washington R*dskins may really believe that their mascot is a "tribute" to Native peoples; they're still walking around with a racial slur on their shirts.

6. "They're not saying that ALL (female, gay, Black, etc.) people are like that, just these specific ones."

This is also known as the "but some women *are* bitches" argument. An artist cannot control how people ingest their art. Interpretations differ. Characters and images in pop culture are always symbols for larger communities, whether or not the creator of that character meant it to be that way. Sure, Long Duk Dong from "16 Candles" is just one specific character. But in a movie (and corresponding cultural landscape) that has no other Asian characters, he becomes a vessel for Asian-ness and Otherness, both of which are characterized negatively. See point #5.

7. Anything involving the phrase "politically correct."

As much as people try to characterize those who are offended as oversensitive whiners, phrases like "PC police" and "I don't believe in political correctness" absolutely reek of "boo hoo I actually have to think about what I'm saying and consider other people's feelings; I'm so oppressed!" Political correctness doesn't mean that you can't be honest. It doesn't mean that you can't be offensive, if that offensive language is making a larger, important point. It just means "don't be a jackass." The "PC police" defense is a blanket rhetorical device that allows thoughtless people to dodge criticism. If you are going to say/ do something offensive, it should serve a greater purpose, and you should take whatever criticism you have coming openly and honestly.

8. Why would you expect something better? They're just trying to make money and most people don't care about this stuff.

Of course this is true. But to simply internalize it is defeatism. We can fight back, make noise, start conversations, engage in boycotts, write articles, create better art, and make the connections between pop culture and society that need to be made.

POP CULTURE, BAD JOKES, AND BULLY CULTURE

Whenever the media catches someone making an offensive joke, saying something hurtful, or doing something insensitive, the same questions get asked, over and over again:

"Was that really offensive, or is everyone just overreacting? Are we too sensitive?"

"Isn't it the job of artists and comedians to push buttons and shake things up?"

"It was just a joke. Why are people so caught up on this little thing, when there are real problems out there?"

These are the wrong questions, and it's time we stopped asking them. Here are three better ones:

Who's making the joke, who's laughing, and who's being laughed at?

When *The Onion* calls 9-year-old Quvenzhané Wallis a c***, I assume they don't really mean it. But I also know that the "joke" taps into a long, painful history of young Black women being dehumanized, devalued, and abused. The "humor" is entirely contingent on people either not knowing or not caring about that.

And this isn't about free speech. Everyone is free to say whatever they want. This is about the choices we have as both creators and consumers of culture. The battle here is not pro-censorship vs. anti-censorship, or the uptight PC police vs. the badass artistic rebels; it's "thoughtless bullies saying hurtful things about historically and institutionally oppressed people for cheap shock value" vs. "people with standards." Which side are you on?

What is the larger point being made with the joke or statement? Is there one?

If you absolutely have to offend someone in order to make some grand philosophical statement about the nature of human existence, fine. But when Lisa Lampanelli uses the n-word to refer to her friend Lena Dunham, or when Daniel Tosh laughs about the idea of a woman in his audience being raped, or when Eminem raps about murdering gay people, or when a NYC assemblyman (or St. Paul police officer, for that matter) wears blackface makeup—what's the reason?

999 times out of a thousand, there isn't one. Even when it's not overtly malicious, it's a tired joke. It's a lazy attempt to come off as edgy when you're not talented enough to actually say something edgy. It's the unholy union of the willfully ignorant and the gleefully privileged, and it adds nothing new or interesting to the larger conversation.

"Edgy" comedy or art shouldn't just be about saying naughty words and pissing people off; it should be about pissing people off in order to make a larger point.

I'm not against any kind of joke on principle. A good comic can make anything funny. But if you're going to make jokes about rape, your excuse has to be something more than "it's okay to hurt people because the bit landed, it was funny." If you're going to make jokes about potentially offensive topics, there's an easy way and a hard way. The easy way is to just shout out offensive things in the name of free speech and "pushing people out of their comfort zones." The hard way is to provide an unflinching, in-depth analysis of the way that people deal with these painful topics, to really explore them, in order to make some kind of profound point about them (and be funny).

Most people who make rape jokes (or gay jokes, or racist jokes, and so on) aren't smart enough to have anything worthwhile to add to the conversation. They're hacks. It's like a little kid shouting "poop!" in the grocery store and then grinning. Truly edgy writing pushes people out of their comfort zones, sure. But it pushes them toward something, some deeper truth or observation about humanity.

What is the relationship between these so-called "little things" and the "real problems" of the world?

Every time a rapper says the word "bitch," even if they're not using it in an explicitly misogynistic way; every time a college student dresses up in a Halloween costume that is a caricature of someone else's culture; every time some hipster says something racist to prove how "beyond race" they are; every time you post a Facebook status talking about how a particularly tough video game is "raping" you—none of these things alone represent the end of the world. It's about the cumulative effect.

Language impacts thought; thought impacts action. And when our language is so casually cruel, when it normalizes what should be offensive, when it sacrifices empathy and critical thought for the cheap sugar rush of breaking taboos or getting a chuckle out of your audience—that affects the real world. That hurts people. That is the bullshit that fertilizes the ground from which oppression, inequality, bigotry, and hate grow.

Imagine you're in high school. Every day, you witness a classmate subjected to a hundred "little things" from other students: a light shove in the hallway, a name-called in the lunchroom, hateful graffiti on a locker, taunting over Facebook, spitballs in the back of the head, etc. Any of those things by themselves might be manageable. But all of them, together, day after day after day—they add up.

And sure, you could tell the student to "get over himself" and "stop being so sensitive." Or you could stand with him, as an ally, and refuse to be yet another bully. The choice is yours.

WHEN YOU HATE THAT YOU LOVE A PIECE OF ART OR POP CULTURE

The first rap group that I really fell in love with was Goodie Mob. If you only know Cee-lo as a reality TV star, or as the singer in Gnarls Barkley, it's important to understand that Cee-lo, as a member of Goodie Mob, was one of the best MCs ever. I learned how to rap by listening to Cee-lo (not to mention the very underrated Big Gipp), and the group's first two albums are southern hip hop classics.

It was not until I was years out of high school that I noticed a couple of Goodie Mob lines (not from Cee-lo, but from group member Khujo) that were explicitly, inarguably, violently homophobic. Maybe I was just too young and ignorant to understand them before, but I suddenly had to see the group in a very different light.

I know I'm not alone in this. Maybe you grew up watching Buffy, and then suddenly noticed how few fleshed-out characters of color there are in Joss Whedon's work. Maybe you really like Game of Thrones, but feel uncomfortable with some of the weird gender and race stuff in the series. Maybe you think Robin Thicke's new song is the song of the year, but also think that the lyrics are incredibly problematic. How do we reconcile all this stuff?

First things first: I don't claim to have the answers. But here are a few points I try to keep in mind:

We can and should be critical of the things we love
Being a fan of something isn't an all-or-nothing proposition. It's not "I like this, so I'm going to turn my brain off," or "this is offensive so it's automatically terrible." Culture is more complex than that. We like what we like. As individuals, however, we should be able to develop a critical eye and understand how even some of the art that we love has problematic elements.

We should be able to have conversations about it without getting defensive. We should be able to make connections between the pop culture we consume and the society in which we live.

...at the same time, there has to be a line

It's easy to take that last point and use it as a rationalization to never be truly critical of anything, like "yeah this neo-Nazi folk music is terrible, but it has such pretty melodies!" It's okay—and healthy—to draw lines, to choose not to be a part of something. The common argument of "if you don't like it, don't listen to it" is usually a cop-out response meant to shut down debate, but it can also be a survival mechanism.

Drawing "the line" is going to be an ongoing struggle for everyone, but it's good to remember that if something is rubbing you the wrong way, there are millions upon millions of other songs, books, shows, and movies out there to be experiencing.

There's a difference between what we enjoy and what we promote/support

For example, you can listen to Eminem without buying any of his music, posting about him on social media or telling anyone about how much you like him. You don't have to put money in his—or his label's—pockets. We all probably have a DVD or an album in our collection that doesn't exactly line up with the social justice values and principles we believe in. That doesn't make you a hypocrite. That doesn't make you a bad person. The important thing is to strive to understand your feelings, continue navigating the aforementioned "line," and keep fighting for those values and principles in your everyday life. Again, don't shut your brain off; keep trying to cultivate awareness and action.

...at the same time, everything that we ingest has an impact

Just something to keep in mind: whether it affects us at a conscious, rational level or a deeper level, art is like food. If you ingest too much crap, it's going to have negative consequences, one way or another.

Cultivating awareness and a critical eye/ear doesn't ruin art; it makes it better

I can't go to movies on a whim any more. The sexism, the racism, the homophobia, not to mention the general wackness of 90% of everything Hollywood releases just doesn't appeal to me. But it also makes the good movies, when they come along, that much more enjoyable. When you finally find a piece of art that speaks to you as art, but also isn't brought down by stereotypical characters, or offensive ideas, or lack of representation– that's a beautiful feeling. The same is true for TV, books, poetry, music and other forms of culture and communication.

Do I still listen to Goodie Mob sometimes? Sure. But it's a complex experience. It's not just "this song is good;" it's an ongoing internal conversation about the roots of oppression, about the responsibilities of an artist, about my own life, privileges, and experiences, and how they line up with the ideas being expressed in the songs. It's not as simple as just sitting back and vibing out to some music, but that's okay.

Pop culture isn't just escapism; it's our mythology, our hive mind's currents and undercurrents. A little active listening is healthy. It can even be fun.

MAYBE PROGRESSIVES ARE TOO CRITICAL OF EACH OTHER, OR MAYBE YOU'RE JUST NOT USED TO BEING CRITICIZED

"The Left is eating itself!"

"We need to focus on our real enemies instead of criticizing each other!"

"Ultra radical social justice warriors are a joke, and their PC-policing will be the end of the progressive movement!"

There was a time when I was a lot more sympathetic to attitudes like this (well, at least the first two). If you're around activists, online and offline, you do start to notice a particular breed of organizer who seems to care more about scoring more-radical-than-thou points than about actually building a movement. They might roll their eyes because you haven't read a particular book, or talk all in academic jargon and then be super condescending when you don't get what they're saying, or swoop in to point out what you did wrong while never actually pitching in.

And yeah, those people are annoying. But they're also relatively rare. The problem is that there seems to be a growing number of progressives who take that basic posture archetype and apply it to anyone who has a critique, or a call for greater inclusiveness, or a challenge to the progressive status quo. So even when people have super legitimate, necessary critiques, they get lumped in with the fringe, characterized as "just as bad" as their radical conservative counterparts.

The reason that I'm no longer sympathetic to those attitudes is that my real-life experience with movement-building has shown me that very rarely is the problem that progressives are too critical; much more often, we are not critical enough.

When Bernie Sanders flubs an opportunity to stand with the #BlackLivesMatter movement, we can acknowledge that as a flub and push him (and his relentlessly white campaign) to do better, or we can shout down the critiques, on some *"he's really great and the best chance we have for real change so everyone shut up!"*

When a panel discussion on a feminist issue features five white women, and then gets called out for being too white, that's not "nitpicking." That's acknowledging the long tradition of the erasure of indigenous women and women of color from mainstream feminist discourse, and pushing for something better. Maybe it's easier to see it as "not a big deal" when you happen to not be affected by it.

When "well-meaning" talk-show hosts and journalists continue to ask ridiculous, offensive, invasive questions to trans people, we shouldn't all just shut up because they're "trying to raise awareness." There are ways to raise awareness without throwing people's dignity under the bus. Again, they can do better.

The whole "we have to stop making good the enemy of perfect" attitude assumes that those adjectives are objective and universal, ignoring the fact that what so many of us see as "good" can actually be harmful and counterproductive to movement-building efforts. Historically, who has been able to frame this debate and decide what "good" is anyway? Even in progressive circles, it's been people who already have some access to power.

So now, when the internet gives a platform to counter-narratives and other definitions of "good," old-school mainstream liberals find themselves being challenged. That's why so much of this discourse is couched in condescending, tech-oriented language ("hashtag activist," "tumblr feminist," etc.), and framed as personal attacks when they're actually critiques of power.

The idea that feminism, for example, has been "taken over" by the *man-hating trigger warning reverse racist thought police* is as ridiculous as it is weirdly common, and a lot of the people making that argument either benefit from the status quo, or have no dog in the fight anyway. My job lets me meet feminists, activists, and leftists from all over, and I can tell you: the problem isn't that "we're too self-critical." A lot more damage is done by those with some access to power refusing to be challenged/critiqued than by the critics themselves.

The thing that I just cannot wrap my head around is this bizarre belief that it's so *hard*, that there's an expectation that everyone has to be *perfect* and we just can't—as individuals or as a movement— ever get there. Everyone makes mistakes. No one is perfect. But there is an enormous difference between those of us who actively *try* to do better and those of us who whine and want the rest of the movement to accept us unconditionally.

I'm certainly not perfect, but somehow, even as a very vocal, very privileged, public personality talking about a lot of serious issues, my life is not an endless series of call-outs.

If your life *does* seem like an endless series of call-outs, maybe that's on *you*. If you're a liberal professor and you're scared of your liberal students because they embody "call-out culture," maybe you deserve to get called out because you're saying or doing things that hurt people.

If you're a guy who doesn't feel welcome in feminist circles, maybe you should think about why you want to be in feminist circles as opposed to introducing feminist ideals into the circles you're already part of. If you're working on a campaign and you know that your candidate's platform will have a positive effect on communities of color, but those communities aren't supporting you, maybe you need to do more to bridge that gap rather than huff and puff that "they" just don't get it. Of course, passionate people go too far sometimes. But it's really important to think critically about who gets to define "too far."

Because for every bogeyman story about someone caught up in a wave of critique for an honest mistake or misunderstanding, there are many, many more stories about erasure, invisibility, and liberal racism/sexism/homophobia/etc. that have been silenced for decades. Slowly, this is changing. This shift is happening right now, and as progressives, we should have the strategic and moral sense to embrace it.

To me, being a progressive/radical/leftist means challenging established systems of power. Doing that within our own movement doesn't make us weaker when it comes to doing that in our society; everything I've ever learned or experienced as an activist tells me that it makes us immeasurably stronger, and that it's the only way we can actually win.

EVERYTHING ELSE: AN EXCLUSIVE INTERVIEW WITH GUANTE

Conducted by Guante, because this is all just a structural conceit for me to share a few random thoughts and answers to common questions in a form that isn't just another essay or op-ed.

Thank you for sitting down with me today, and thank you for buying lunch—for me, and for everyone in the restaurant today.

No problem. I'm great.

Let's start with the title. "A Love Song, A Death Rattle, A Battle Cry" is from your song "The National Anthem." But is there any further significance behind choosing that to title what is, in many ways, the capstone to your career up until this point?

I think art is about balancing intentionality with luck. You plan, you coordinate, and you think critically about your audience and your message, but at the end of the day, there is always an element of chance—people interpret the message of a poem differently from your intention, or something happens in the world that changes the meaning of a particular line, or you look like hell on the day you're scheduled to shoot the video, etc.

With the title of this project, I picked it because it sounded cool. That's it. But as I got deeper into putting everything together, the spirit of the project really illuminated those words in a new way.

Like a lot of artists, I want to create work that doesn't fit neatly into boxes, work that surprises and challenges the listener. I don't always actually do that, but that's the guiding principle. For me, work that is *all* substance, all Grand Political Statements, is always going to feel manipulative or preachy. Work that is *all* craft and technical brilliance is always going to feel hollow. And work that is *all* raw, uncut expression is always going to feel unfinished.

I'm not saying anything revolutionary here, but the key is balancing those three impulses. I want to create work that is grounded in real-life experience and has a human element. I want to create work that pushes boundaries and has an edge to it. I want to create work that says something meaningful. And I want to do all of that at once. A love song, a death rattle, a battle cry. It wasn't an intentional metaphor, but when I figured that out, it just clicked.

If balancing those three elements is your general goal as an artist, do you have any more specific goals? What do you want your art to do?

Art is a weapon, not the war. I don't believe that my job as an artist is to make the "best" art I am capable of making. I believe that it is to add something meaningful to the larger conversation, and also that that "conversation" is bigger than art.

I view my work not as some kind of mystical, magical expression of my individual soul; I just see it as another way to communicate and engage with my community. Art is an opportunity to have conversations we don't usually get to have, to frame issues or ideas in new and compelling ways, to help guide and shape long-term cultural changes, and to bring people together to create physical space for community and connection.

Of course, striving to be more technically proficient with your craft is a good thing, and I'm not saying "it doesn't matter how talented you are as long as you're saying something meaningful." It absolutely does matter how talented you are, and I think pretending like it doesn't is counterproductive. Talent opens doors; it makes our raw expression more sustainable and further-reaching. But talent is a tool, a means to an end.

I've just seen too many artists limit themselves by believing that their art is all they have to offer. I've seen too many aspiring talents focus so much of their energy on fitting into some mold of what an artist is "supposed to be" that they're never able to develop their own voices and perspectives. This is like having the sharpest sword but not being present at the battle.

So to answer the question more directly, I want my art to be transformative. And some of that may come from the art itself, like if someone hears "Cherry Spoon Bridge to Nowhere" and begins to think differently about how they move through their scene. But I think that transformation is much more likely to come through the *space* that the art creates.

I want to continue to help make platforms for young people to create their own art. I want to use my position as an artist to connect people and organizations doing good work. I want to use the networks I've built as an artist to signal-boost causes that are important to me. I want to organize events that put people in the room together who would otherwise not be in the room together.

I want to use my art to open up real conversations about larger social justice concepts.

All of that, to me, is why art is powerful. And that's what I'd like mine to do.

Social justice has always been a big part of your work. How do you see art fitting into a social/political movement framework?

When I was very young, I thought that writing a poem about war could end war. Clearly, that's a naïve position. So as I started engaging more with both art and activism, I wanted to distance myself from that past naiveté, so I swung to the other extreme and completely separated the two: I worked on my art, and I did "activist stuff," but I didn't put them together in any meaningful way.

Today, a word that I've fallen in love with is "synergy." I stand by my position that art by itself is not powerful enough to change much. But art organically integrated into a campaign, art as a supplementary force in a larger movement, art as a way to frame and engage with the work that organizers do—these can all be incredibly powerful.

Art isn't just about having music at the rally, or writing a poem about a political issue; it's a lens through which we can view organizing in a more holistic way. Artistic approaches can be infused into movements at every level—from valuing and validating our stories, to creating websites and promotional materials that are aesthetically engaging, to exploring new networks and avenues for reaching out to potential allies—the list goes on.

Art has the power to frame arguments and issues in a way that is down-to-earth and understandable. It can put a human face on big, abstract ideas. We've seen how powerful storytelling can be in a movement setting. Our narratives matter, sometimes even more than our statistics and logical arguments.

Add to this everything I talked about in the last question about art having the power to create physical spaces and bring people together, and I think it's clear that the relationship between art and politics is much bigger, and much more powerful, than simply art *about* politics.

Are there any examples of how this plays out in real life?

My favorite example is probably the SNCC Freedom Singers, who would sing to inspire marchers during the Civil Rights Movement; in a sense, it's not about the song—it's about the act of singing, about the environment that that song can create. Their art got people ready to face dogs, firehouses, and police brutality—even the prospect of death.

A more recent example is the hip hop group the Figureheads, who have used hip hop to create programming for children with developmental disabilities. I also look at artists like I Self Devine, Bao Phi, Tish Jones, Ricardo Levins Morales, Tou SaiKo Lee and many others who have successfully integrated arts practices into real, concrete community activism.

The current spoken word movement in general fits in here as well. I want young people to write good poems, but I also know that "writing good poems" is always secondary to critical thinking, exploring their identities, talking about the issues that are important to them, being validated for their opinions, and just getting together and having fun.

With all of that in mind, what do you feel that you've accomplished in the past five years?

That's a complicated question. Part of me wants to say "not much," quite frankly. I know I've done a lot of good work, but I also know that that good work was more about building for the future than accomplishing anything concrete in the present.

I mean, I've facilitated hundreds of workshops and classes on social justice issues like identity, privilege, and power, as well as arts-related issues like telling your story, integrating the arts into activism, and more. I know that education is important, and that it has a ripple effect, that a single educator may never really see the fruits of their labor. I also know that I've done a lot of stuff we talked about in the last few questions, in terms of using my art and my position as an artist to open up spaces, signal-boost other voices, etc. So I shouldn't say that I haven't accomplished anything.

But this is also about perspective. I look up to people who aim big. So my somewhat subdued response here may be less about discontent with the past and more about excitement for the future.

It's really easy to say that you're "doing good work." I need to challenge myself not to do good work, which I'm doing anyway, but to have the maximum impact I can possibly have in the time that I have. And with that as the metric, I've probably come up short. But the struggle continues.

To you, where does lasting change come from?

I've always broken it down into four areas; this is just a framework that helps me wrap my head around how change happens and how I fit into it:

- Change happens on a personal level (educating ourselves, engaging in critical self-analysis, reading books, taking classes, being intentional about the language we use, making good consumer choices, etc.)

- Change happens on an interpersonal level (having conversations with friends and family about social/political issues, writing blogs and social media posts, engaging with art/media in any capacity, teaching, direct service activism, volunteering, etc.)

- Change happens on an institutional level (organizing and activism—rallies, marches, sit-ins, etc.; as well as voting and electoral politics; whatever can be done to create sustainable policy change and fundamentally shift how institutions are structured)

- Change happens on a cultural level (long-term, "hearts and minds" change)

For me, the key is simultaneity; we need all four of these levels to be happening at once. One or two at a time isn't sustainable or effective. Like the saying goes "thought without action is a daydream; action without thought is a nightmare."

Art very clearly fits into the interpersonal change level, in terms of how we use art to have conversations and transmit ideas. It also fits into the cultural change level, in terms of how attitudes shift over time. This framework also illustrates, however, how art by itself, divorced from a movement context (at the institutional change level) isn't enough. We need all four levels for change to really happen.

The challenge is to figure out where you, as an individual, fit into this framework. That's what the poem "Starfish" is about. That's what the song "The Hero" is about. Because sometimes there's tension. Sometimes you know that you're doing good work and you know that it's not enough. Or sometimes you're fighting for something so big and abstract that you feel disconnected. But I think these are the things we have to grapple with if we care about creating change.

On a more positive note, this model also shows how there's always *something* that we can do. Just because we don't have the power to run out the door and immediately make everything perfect, it doesn't mean that we don't have power.

Between your video series sharing tips for aspiring spoken word poets, a bunch of essays sharing advice and resources with young artists, and your actual work with teens, it seems like "giving back" is important to you. Why is that?

Both spoken word and hip hop exist in communities where passing on information and resources to the next generation isn't just a tradition, it's a necessity. You don't get an MFA in rapping. You don't get some huge grant to rock a party. We learn from each other. I'm sure that that cooperative spirit isn't the same every where, but it's always been a huge part of the communities through which I move.

Again, though, it's also about synergy. I get paid to work with youth. Having multiple revenue streams has been a key component of my being able to sustain myself as an artist full-time. It's a win-win.

Related to that point, if you had to condense all of those "advice to young artists" pieces into a handful of paragraphs, what would be the most vital points?

I guess number one would be to define success for yourself, and set concrete, actionable goals based on that definition. It's so easy to just drift along and see what happens. And there's nothing necessarily wrong with that; if your definition of success is simply to have fun and make some art, that's beautiful. But if you have more specific goals, it takes planning and intentionality.

On a super concrete level, that means being organized. Keep a calendar. Make to-do lists. Respond to emails right away. Show up to things on time. It's one thing to have a philosophy in place; it's something else to actually follow through on it. Some of these so-called little things end up being extremely important.

Number two would be to recognize that it is no great victory to be talented. Millions of people are talented. Talent is a spectrum, and there will always be some people on either side of you. So work on your craft, try to get better at what you do, sure; but the real challenge is to develop a unique voice, to add something original to the larger conversation. To me, a creative, ambitious failure is always more valuable than a perfectly-executed paint-by-numbers piece of art.

A phenomenally skilled MC, for example, gets a B+ in my book. To get an A or an A+, you have to be a phenomenally skilled MC who actually has something unique or meaningful or interesting to say.

Number three is related to that; it's to remember that the most powerful art doesn't necessarily come from the most talented artists. It comes from people who experience their world and meaningfully engage with their communities. You don't have to lock yourself up in a cabin for six months to write a great novel. A better approach is to go to events, join organizations, network with people, perform at open mics, read books, start a writing circle, have fun, work hard— live your life—and then write about it.

Building off that, number four would be to actively and intentionally promote yourself. Don't be obnoxious and just spam people, obviously, but do take yourself seriously and work to get your art—that you presumably care about—heard by as many people as possible. Unless you're already a world-famous writer with a million-dollar agent, making great art is the first step, not the last one.

Finally, keeping in mind that there are a million tips, tactics, and tools we could potentially talk about here, I'd just say to work together. Collaborate. I believe that communities cultivate great art, not just individuals. So find a writing circle, or an online forum, or an open mic, or an after-school club, and build with each other.

That's it?

Oh and don't be a jerk. That's an important one. Watch the other acts on the bill. Be nice to the sound technicians. Cultivate a sense of humor.

What keeps drawing you back to spoken word?

I always tell students, with spoken word, you can say whatever you want to say, however you want to say it. That complete freedom can be intimidating, but it can also be incredibly liberating once you wrap your head around it. There are no limits. There are traditions, tropes, etc., but there really are no rules. It's one kind of art that can still be legitimately shocking.

But even beyond the fun of writing and performing spoken word, I believe in the larger movement. This is about democratizing the arts. This is about people—especially people who traditionally don't have access to "high art" spaces—creating a platform to not only take part in the world of poetry, but really take it over. That is incredibly exciting.

Along those same lines, what keeps drawing you back to hip hop?

I want to talk about community, about friendships, and about how it's such an exciting time for hip hop—both here in the Twin Cities and everywhere. But my honest answer to that question has more to do with writing and the process of creating songs. Writing rhymes over music is just magic. I feel like all of my best poems are songs.

A few bonus questions pulled from social media and awkward post-show conversations with people:

Why the name "Guante?"

I did not choose the name; it's a high school nickname that I just kind of got stuck with. The rest is a long story. I will say, however, that I've tried to be really careful to not use the name in any kind of advantageous way; I'm mixed, but I'm not Latino. So on a super basic level, the name is appropriative, and it's important to me to act in ways that push back against any potential exploitative uses of it. If someone wants to pay me a bunch of money to play their Latinx heritage festival or something, I'm always going to say no, and always going to recommend a half-dozen other artists I know who are Latinx.

I may start to phase the handle out, actually. This book is credited to *Kyle "Guante" Tran Myhre*, which I've been using more and more. Someday it might just be *Kyle Tran Myhre*. I'm open to other suggestions.

Why the black hat?

THE BLACK HAT IS SYMBOLIC OF THE NIGHT SKY THROUGH WHICH OUR ANCESTORS VOYAGED, THE CONCAVE/CONVEX WARMTH OF ABSOLUTE EMPTINESS, THE VAST NOTHINGNESS TO WHICH WE SHALL INEVITABLY RETURN.

Okay. What do your tattoos mean?

I have a song about that. You can listen to it on my SoundCloud.

What's your favorite song of yours? Favorite poem?

First would be "Matches," which I think is the perfect encapsulation of my philosophy and personality. Second is a toss-up between "Asterisk" and "Revolver." I don't have a lot of pretty songs, but I'm a sucker for pretty songs.

As for poems, I love performing the zombie one, because even though it's silly on a literal level, it's one of the more honest, heartfelt things I've written. But "The Family Business" is probably my all-around favorite.

Finally, what's next for you?

Answering this is tricky, because it's not just a blog post I can delete later if I change my mind. But as of this very movement, I just finished grad school at the University of Minnesota. My program was an interdisciplinary look at how spoken word can be used to make social justice education programs more critical.

So I'm looking at things like first-year orientation programs, bystander intervention programs, those mandatory "diversity trainings" that everyone hates, stuff like that, and trying to apply spoken word (as both a specific thing and a broader cultural practice) in order to make them align more with the principles of critical pedagogy. Making these programs more critical is the key to moving beyond "talking about our privilege" and actually allocating resources to change systems and institutions, and I think that spoken word offers a compelling entry point into that process. This is also pretty much the work that I do day-to-day, when I travel to colleges around the country performing poems and facilitating dialogue based on those poems.

I could go on. But maybe that'll be the next book.

I'm also working on doing more work with poetry over music—not rapping, not doing a capella slam-style pieces—just pushing myself out of my comfort zone. Lots of other projects (especially collaborative projects) are on the horizon too, but that's a good snapshot of where my head is at right now.

How can people keep in touch with you?

When I ask people to follow me on Twitter, or like the Guante page on Facebook, it's important to me that I communicate that that's about something more than numbers and ego. I really believe in the power of social media. I genuinely want to stay connected to the people who like my work.

Also, I try to use my website as a central hub for a ton of resources— it's not just the place to find my music and spoken word videos; it's also full of lists, links and what I hope are helpful tools for artists and activists. Check it out:

www.guante.info
www.twitter.com/elguante
www.facebook.com/guantesolo
www.instagram.com/guantesolo
www.youtube.com/tripguante
www.guante.tumblr.com

And thank you!

.

ACKNOWLEDGEMENTS

Family, friends, fans, anyone who pays attention—thanks. I know everyone says this, but there really are too many people to thank here. But here are a few:

Sha and e.g. for helping me make the jump.

See More, Spencer, Graham, Claire, Chastity, Lydia, Kristoff, Josh, Rube, Desmond, Dan, Ganzo, and everyone else I've ever worked with for making me sound good. There are more, of course, but these people are all on the album that goes along with this book.

Tish Jones and the whole TruArtSpeaks family for being role models.

Button Poetry for the massive signal boost.

The entire Twin Cities hip hop community for being more than it has to be.

The entire Twin Cities spoken word community for pushing boundaries.

The entire Twin Cities activist/social justice community for making a difference.

Family and friends for the unconditional support.

UTM and Yoshi for everything.

ABOUT THE AUTHOR

Kyle "Guante" Tran Myhre is an MC, two-time National Poetry Slam champion, activist and educator based in Minneapolis, MN. His work has appeared everywhere from the United Nations, to Welcome to Night Vale, to Upworthy and beyond, and he currently makes a living traveling to colleges, conferences, and high schools, using spoken word as a jumping-off point for dialogue around identity, power, agency, and activism.

OTHER BOOKS BY BUTTON POETRY

If you enjoyed this book, please consider checking out some of our others, below. Readers like you allow us to keep broadcasting and publishing. Thank you!

Aziza Barnes, *me Aunt Jemima and the nailgun.*

J. Scott Brownlee, *Highway or Belief*

Nate Marshall, *Blood Percussion*

Sam Sax, *A Guide to Undressing Your Monsters*

Mahogany L. Browne, *smudge*

Neil Hilborn, *Our Numbered Days*

Sierra DeMulder, *We Slept Here*

Danez Smith, *black movie*

Cameron Awkward-Rich, *Transit*

Jacqui Germain, *When the Ghosts Come Ashore*

Hanif Willis-Abdurraqib, *The Crown Ain't Worth Much*

Aaron Coleman, *On Trigger*

Olivia Gatwood, *New American Best Friend*

Donte Collins, *Autopsy*

Melissa Lozada-Oliva, *peluda*

William Evans, *Still Can't Do My Daughter's Hair*

Rudy Francisco, *Helium*

Available at buttonpoetry.com/shop and more!